The Civilian Rights Handguide
A Citizen's Guide to Navigating Police Encounters

Disclaimer

Nothing in this book should be construed as legal advice. Seek the services of a legal professional if you require legal councel. The topics covered in this book are designed to be educational and informative and *should not serve as legal advice under any circumstances.*

 Prism Publishing

ISBN
Paperback: 979-8-9920143-0-3
Hardcover: 979-8-9920143-2-7
Ebook: 979-8-9920143-1-0

The Civilian Rights Handguide

A CITIZEN'S GUIDE TO NAVIGATING POLICE ENCOUNTERS

John Lang

Table of Contents

Introduction. i

1. The Constitution and The Courts 1
   The Constitution and Civilian Rights. 7
   Courts and the Judicial System 22
2. The Foundation of Freedom 31
   Search and Seizure. 32
   The Warrant Requirement 42
   Public Property and Private Property 57
3. Reasonable Suspicion and Probable Cause 62
   Reasonable Suspicion Recap 77
   Probable Cause. 79
4. Detainment and Arrest. 82
   Investigative Detentions. 83
   Traffic Stops 88
   Arrests 96
   Excessive Force 104
5. The Right to Remain Silent 110
   Invoking the Right to Remain Silent. 112
   Police Questioning: How to Respond 115
   Use The Fifth Amendment Wisely 119
   The Miranda Warning 123
   Compelled Statements and Legal Obligations 128
6. Standing Up for Your Rights 132
   Staying Calm Under Stress 132
   The Psychology of Police Encounters 135
   When and How to Comply 142
   The Reality of Police Deception 146
   The Prevalence of Uneventful Police Encounters 151
7. Encountering Police in Public 157
   When can the police stop you in public? 157
   When can the police ask for ID? 161
   When can the police search you? 163
   Can you record your encounter? 165
   Can the police take your phone? 166
   Are police officers required to identify themselves? 168

Can you request a supervisor? 169
Can an officer stop you outside their jurisdiction? 170
8. Encountering Police on the Road 172
How to Avoid a Traffic Stop 173
What to Do When Being Pulled Over 175
Vehicle Searches. 178
What is a citation? 181
Can the police order you out of your vehicle? 182
Is there a time limit to traffic stops? 183
When can the police use a canine? 184
DUI Checkpoints 186
9. Encountering Police at Home 190
Do the police need a warrant to enter your property? 191
Do you have Fourth Amendment rights as a tenant? 194
Welfare Checks. 196
What to Do if the Police Knock on Your Door. 198
10. What to Do After an Encounter. 202
Immediate Action Post-Encounter .203
Navigating an Arrest. 207
Filing a Complaint 211
Filing a FOIA request 216
Seeking Legal Representation 221
Understanding Police Liability 227
Resources for Deeper Understanding 232

Introduction

For the average citizen, police interactions are a relatively foreign experience. Despite the fact that nearly every American will come into contact with police officers at some point in their lives, many citizens are completely unprepared to handle any kind of police interaction, and rightfully so.

A well known concept in psychology known as "normalcy bias" explains that people tend to underestimate the possibility of a disaster or adverse event occurring simply because it hasn't happened to them before. This bias leads people to assume that things will continue as they always have, causing them to dismiss warnings and fail to prepare for potential risks. The mindset is rooted in the belief that since something has never happened before, it won't happen in the future, despite evidence or indications to the contrary.

For example, a person might think, "I've never had any problems with the police before, so I don't need to worry about knowing my rights in detail." This complacency can leave them unprepared for unexpected situations where a thorough understanding of their rights could be crucial.

By proactively learning about your rights and proper procedures during police interactions, you position yourself to respond effectively if such a situation arises. This preparation doesn't mean living in fear of negative events, but rather acknowledging that they are within the realm of possibility and taking reasonable steps to be prepared. Understanding normalcy bias highlights the importance of not letting complacency deter you from taking actions that protect your interests.

The importance of understanding our rights extends beyond individual encounters; it has profound implications for society as a whole. When citizens are knowledgeable about their legal protections, they serve as a check against the misuse of authority. This collective awareness fosters accountability and encourages law enforcement to adhere to legal standards and ethical practices. In essence, an informed populace helps maintain the delicate balance of power between the government and the people. This balance is absolutely essential for the functioning of a healthy democracy.

Reflecting on history, we see numerous examples where the erosion of individual liberties has led to the rise of oppressive regimes. When a society becomes complacent about its rights, or worse, ignorant of them, it opens the door to abuses of power that can dismantle the very foundations of freedom. The stories of authoritarian states often begin with the gradual encroachment on personal liberties, justified under the guise of security or order, and facilitated by a populace that is either uninformed or apathetic.

Understanding our rights is not merely an academic exercise;

it is a fundamental aspect of our participation in a free and just society. The philosophical underpinnings of individual liberty are deeply intertwined with the concept of "the rule of law." The rule of law asserts that every person is subject to the law, including lawmakers and enforcers, ensuring fairness and equality.

When citizens are informed about their rights, they are better equipped to hold institutions accountable, reinforcing the rule of law. Conversely, a society that neglects the education of its citizens in legal matters risks sliding into a state where laws are applied arbitrarily, and justice becomes a privilege rather than a guarantee. Education about constitutional rights encourages citizens to engage with societal issues, participate in democratic processes, and advocate for reforms when necessary.

Being knowledgeable about your rights is also a form of self-respect and personal empowerment. It affirms your dignity as an individual and your role as an active participant in society. This self-assuredness can influence how you carry yourself in various situations, and can potentially project a level of confidence that deters violations of your rights. It also enables you to assist others who may be less informed, and foster a supportive community where people look out for one another.

In practical terms, understanding your rights can also de-escalate potentially tense situations, help you avoid unnecessary legal troubles, and potentially save your life. Being aware of legal procedures and protocols allows you to recognize when they are not being followed, and enables you to take appropriate action afterward, such as filing a complaint or seeking legal counsel. Knowing your rights empowers you to make informed decisions, protect yourself from potential abuses of power, and contribute to the preservation of civil liberties that form the bedrock of a democratic society.

The presence of law enforcement is woven into the fabric of our daily lives, often unnoticed until a moment of crisis arises. Police officers are entrusted with the vital task of maintaining public order, safeguarding citizens, and upholding the laws that reflect our collective values. Philosophically, the existence of police reflects our collective agreement to abide by certain rules for the greater good. Laws are not merely edicts imposed from above; they are manifestations of societal norms and ethics that have evolved over time.

The police embody the enforcement of these laws, ensuring that the principles we uphold, such as justice, equality, and respect for others, are not just ideals but practical realities. They serve as a bridge between abstract legal concepts and everyday life, and ensure that the rights enshrined in our legal system are protected. However, the power entrusted to law enforcement comes with substantial responsibility. This authority is balanced by the expectation that they will act with integrity, fairness, and respect for the rights of all individuals, but, as you likely know, this is not always the case.

Law enforcement officers are granted significant power to enforce laws, maintain order, and protect citizens. This authority is based on the social contract where citizens cede certain freedoms in exchange for security and justice. When officers misuse their power, it constitutes a breach of this contract, undermining the legitimacy of the legal system and the moral authority of the police. This erosion of trust can lead to a cycle of skepticism and hostility between the public and law enforcement.

For communities disproportionately affected by misconduct, the impact is even more severe. Marginalized groups may experience heightened fear and distrust, and a sense that the very institutions meant to protect them are a source of harm. This can result in reduced cooperation with police investigations, reluctance to report crimes, and a general breakdown in community-police relations. Such dynamics not only hinder effective policing, but also compromise public safety.

The prevalence of misconduct has also prompted calls for systemic reforms. Initiatives like implementing body-worn cameras, revising use-of-force policies, enhancing training on de-escalation techniques, and establishing independent oversight committees demonstrate efforts to increase transparency and accountability.

While this book aims to give you the knowledge to handle police interactions effectively, it's also important to recognize that our legal system has its flaws. Defending yourself against criminal charges can be very expensive, and taking legal action to address wrongdoings by the police can be an even bigger financial burden. When I suggest that battles against police misconduct should be fought in the courtroom, it is with the understanding that, as of right now, this is the only viable avenue for victims of misconduct to seek compensation and accountability.

To be fully prepared for encounters with law enforcement, you need to think about not just the immediate interaction but also the legal processes that might follow. I understand that the costs and difficulties of accessing legal help make this option out of reach for many people, which is a sad reality that highlights socio economic problems within our justice system. These issues show disparities that deserve attention and change, but this book isn't meant to push for systemic reform or to delve into the economic factors that affect access to justice. Instead, this book is intended to serve as a practical guide that presents pertinent facts, laws, court rulings, and legal concepts as they are currently understood.

By providing a clear and comprehensive understanding of the legal landscape as it exists today, my goal is to empower everyday citizens with the tools they need to be safe and informed during police encounters. This knowledge will help you navigate the system more effectively, assert your rights confidently, and make informed decisions anytime you deal with the police. While acknowledging our justice system's flaws, the focus of this book remains on offering actionable guidance to help you protect your interests within the existing legal framework, not advocate for its change or support its current structure.

Although it is important to be prepared for potential challenges during interactions with law enforcement, it is equally crucial to recognize the reality that most police encounters are routine and uneventful. Just as civilians may harbor concerns about encountering an officer who might overstep legal boundaries, police officers often share a parallel apprehension about meeting a civilian who may pose a threat to their safety. Both parties are keenly aware of the rare but serious risks posed to each other, yet these extreme situations are not the norm. Every day, thousands of interactions occur between police officers and citizens that proceed without incident or a violation of rights. These routine encounters are a testament to the professionalism of law enforcement and the general law-abiding nature of the public.

The likelihood of experiencing police misconduct is relatively low when compared to the vast number of daily interactions that conclude peacefully and respectfully. From the officer's perspective, although they are trained to be vigilant for potential dangers, including the rare encounter with a hostile individual, they engage with countless members of the community who are cooperative and pose no threat to their safety.

The reality is that most police officers are dedicated professionals committed to serving and protecting their communities who perform their duties with integrity, and often under challenging circumstances. Similarly, the vast majority of citizens are responsible individuals who respect the law and contribute positively to society. It is important to acknowledge this mutual commitment to civility and order as the foundation of effective community policing and a functioning society.

The purpose of this book is to equip you with knowledge and strategies to navigate police interactions confidently and assert your rights when necessary. While we delve into scenarios involving potential misconduct or constitutional challenges, it is not to suggest that such issues are commonplace. Instead, the goal is to prepare you for exceptional situations, empowering you to handle them appropriately should they arise. By understanding your rights and the legal frameworks that govern police conduct, you can approach interactions with law enforcement from an informed and balanced perspective. Maintaining this perspective helps foster mutual respect between civilians and police officers.

Recognizing that both parties typically seek a peaceful and lawful outcome can alleviate undue anxiety and promote positive engagements. By being informed and prepared, you contribute to a safer environment for yourself and support the broader goal of justice and harmony within the community.

This book intended to serve as a foundational guide for the average citizen, but it is important to recognize that it does not encompass every facet of the complex legal landscape surrounding police interactions. Many of the topics discussed here are vast in scope and have been the subject of extensive scholarly works and dedicated volumes. The aim of this book is to inspire you to delve deeper into the legal system while providing a solid foundation upon which you can build a more comprehensive understanding.

Situations involving police misconduct often require intricate legal knowledge to assess accurately and are best navigated with the assistance of qualified legal professionals. However, possessing a fundamental grasp of your rights as a citizen can be an invaluable asset during any encounter with law enforcement.

Although this guide cannot be, and is not intended to be, a substitute for professional legal advice, the aim is to bridge the gap between complex legal doctrines and everyday experiences. The goal is to make the law accessible and actionable for you, and ultimately helping to foster a more informed and engaged citizenry. Understanding your rights not only protects your individual interests but also contributes to the broader pursuit of justice and accountability within our society as a whole.

Please note that this book is structured into two distinct sections, each designed to guide you through the complexities of police interactions. The first five chapters lay the groundwork by delving deep into the legal framework that governs law enforcement conduct and citizens' rights.

Here, we explore statutes, case law, legal precedents, and the jurisprudence that collectively shape the landscape of police interactions in the United States. This section aims to provide you with a foundational understanding of the legal principles and court decisions that have established the boundaries and responsibilities of both law enforcement and civilians.

Building upon this legal foundation, the subsequent five chapters transition from theory to practice. These chapters focus on how the previously discussed legal concepts directly apply to everyday encounters with the police. By examining real-world scenarios and common situations, we illustrate how legal doctrines manifest in practical terms. This part of the book offers practical advice, strategies, and insights to help you navigate interactions with law enforcement confidently and effectively.

The intent of dividing the book in this manner is to craft a balanced approach that combines an in-depth legal exploration with actionable guidance. This structure is designed to equip you with both the understanding of the laws that govern police conduct and the practical know-how to apply this knowledge in real-life situations. Whether you're seeking to educate yourself on your rights or looking for advice on how to handle specific encounters with law enforcement, this book provides a resource tailored to the needs of the average citizen.

Once you have finished reading this book, I highly recommend taking your legal knowledge a step further by seeking out resources that can offer an even deeper understanding of the legal nuance surrounding police interactions and our justice system. Consider this book one small brick in the foundation of knowledge that you will ultimately build to empower yourself as a citizen and protect yourself, and those you care about, from police misconduct.

Chapter One
The Coustitution and The Courts

When America first announced its independence from Great Britain, there was much debate about how an American government would function on its own. During the Revolutionary War and the years immediately following it, the Thirteen Colonies of America operated as independent nations bound by an agreement to protect one another's sovereignty. No central government truly existed, but each colony was highly dependent upon one another for trading and resources. The Articles of Confederation were eventually drafted to serve as a temporary frame of government, but it did not go into effect until 1781, four years after it was first drafted.

A philosophical debate loomed over the budding country, and the men who were involved in structuring the government of this newly formed society were well aware that their actions would reverberate throughout generations of Americans to come. A temporary form of government no longer supported the needs of the United States once it became its own nation, and it was time for the colonies to decide whether they should remain sovereign or commit to a unified system of government. The country, along with the Founding Fathers, was divided on the issue.

It was clear that America needed a foundational document, but the extent of that document was subject to strong debate. Some argued that the United States needed a constitution to create a federal government that would promote economic growth and ensure that no state took advantage of another. Others opposed the creation of a strong central government, believing that a constitution would undermine the authority of the states, and worried that the position of president might evolve into a monarchy. Many Americans felt as though the country was being stifled by remaining divided and wanted to establish a positive relationship with foreign countries, and they carried the sentiment that America needed a constitution to be taken seriously on the world stage.

Dissenting citizens and representatives refused to allow the constitution to be drafted in a way that would render supreme authority to the federal government and circumvent the principles of individual liberty. Much like in recent years, the country erupted into radical political discourse, and many citizens engaged in acts of protest to demonstrate their political views. Eventually a compromise was reached, and the Bill of Rights was written in an effort to dial back the authority of the federal government and dispel the apprehensions of anti-constitutionalists.

Despite having formed a system that was reluctantly agreed upon by a majority of the state delegates, the Constitution still needed to pass a vote to be ratified. Pennsylvania became the first state to call for an assembly to ratify the Constitution, and, in doing so, also garnered national attention and widespread media coverage. The state was largely populated by citizens who supported the Constitution, but a growing presence of dissenters also resided there, as it was one of the largest, wealthiest, and most influential states in the country.

Pennsylvania representatives called for an assembly on September 29, 1787, but were short of the required votes by two members. A mob formed in the streets of Philadelphia that culminated with two anti-constitutionalists being dragged from their homes and forced to attend the meeting while the assembly voted. It would be another three months before Pennsylvania would officially ratify the Constitution, and another two years before America would officially become "One Nation Under God."

The constitutional dissenters, better known as the anti-federalists, made significant changes to the structure and identity of the Constitution, and played a major role in the development of modern civilian rights and police authority. Their insistence on the inclusion of the Bill of Rights and protections for individual liberty dramatically shaped the political landscape of America, and instilled a sense of individuality that still ripples throughout the fabric of American culture to this very day.

Most Americans have a tentative relationship with the government regardless of whether they are Republican, Democrat, Libertarian, or undecided. According to a 2021 Pew Research Center poll only 22% of Americans say they can trust the government in Washington to do what is right 'most of the time,' with just 2% saying that they can trust the government 'just about always.' The vast majority of Americans readily admit that they do not trust their government, and it could be argued that this skeptical relationship between the citizens and the government of America can be attributed, in some part, to the work of the anti-federalists.

The Bill of Rights became the first ten amendments of the Constitution, and with it established guarantees of personal freedom and individual rights, set clearly defined limitations on the federal government's power in judicial and other proceedings, and explicitly declared that all powers not granted to the government by the Constitution are reserved to the states or the people. These amendments were designed to maintain a balance between the power of the Federal government and the diverse interests of the states, and would go on to form the legal nexus from which officers derive their authority and citizens invoke their rights.

The United States functioned for several years with a loose system of common law enforced by informal private watchmen. It wasn't until 1838 that America established its first police force in Boston. By the 1880s all major U.S. cities had municipal police forces in place that were not composed of volunteers and could be held accountable to a central governmental authority. In the northern states, the need for an organized police force was motivated by growing cities and an increase in petty crimes within those cities. However, the rise of law enforcement in the southern states was largely drawn from managing the slave trade that dominated the region.

The first formal 'Slave Patrol' was created in the Carolina colonies in 1704 and was tasked with maintaining order on large plantations. Prior to the Civil War, many of these vigilante-style organizations existed throughout the southern states, and would evolve into the foundation for the South's police forces once the war had ended. These departments functioned primarily as a means of controlling freed slaves who were now laborers working in an agricultural caste system, as well as enforcing segregation laws.

The source of the South's policing structure would become a major point of focus as the nation began to reform its viewpoint on slavery through the late 1800s. On April 9, 1866, just after the end of the Civil War, the first federal law to define citizenship and affirm that all citizens are equally protected by the law was passed by Congress, and became known as the Civil Rights Act of 1866.

The act accomplished three primary objectives designed to integrate African Americans into mainstream society: to define a citizen as any person born within the United States, to outline the rights guaranteed by this citizenship, and to prohibit the deprivation of any person's citizenship rights "on the basis of race, color, or prior condition of slavery or involuntary servitude." The roots of this act can be traced back to the Emancipation Proclamation, and it was designed to grant the federal government more power to protect the civilian rights of African Americans.

The rise of racially motivated extremists over the years immediately following the passage of the 1866 Act demonstrated a need for further protections. Congress responded relatively quickly with the Enforcement Act of 1871, or better known as the Ku Klux Klan Act. This act was part of three acts that were passed during the Reconstruction Era to protect African Americans from terrorists, like the KKK, and ensure that their right to vote and take part in the political process was cemented into law.

The 1871 Act primarily gave the President the power to detain individuals without the need for a court order in order to combat the KKK and other terrorist organizations, while also acknowledging that government officials were often the ones violating citizens' constitutional rights. At the time, the states had no process for citizens to seek compensation for violations of constitutional protections, and Section 1 of the Enforcement Act of 1871 served as a means to seek monetary relief from state actors who violate a citizen's constitutional rights.

Over the years, Section 1 of the Enforcement Act of 1871 was amended and codified into law under Section 1983 of Title 42 of the United States Code and now states in part:

"Every person who under color of any statute, ordinance, regulation, custom, or usage, of any State or Territory or the District of Columbia, subjects, or causes to be subjected, any citizen of the United States or other person within the jurisdiction thereof to the deprivation of any rights, privileges, or immunities secured by the Constitution and laws, shall be liable to the party injured in an action at law, Suit in equity, or other proper proceeding for redress..."

Today, Section 1983 remains one of the most widely cited laws in cases involving police misconduct, and monetary compensation is a common form of relief for victims of illegal acts committed by members of law enforcement. Section 1983 illustrates one of the many ways that the Constitution, and more specifically the Bill of Rights, has translated into the modern landscape of both policing and civil rights.

While the language of the Constitution appears relatively straightforward when taken at face value, many situations involving police-citizen encounters contain highly specific variables that are not addressed by a plain reading of the

6

document, and it is the justice system's responsibility to interpret the Constitution and apply its logic through courts. The Constitution guarantees all citizens certain unalienable rights, but it is ultimately the duty of the courts to determine when, where, and how those rights are protected.

Interpreting the antiquated language of the Constitution and applying it to modern police encounters often requires a case-by-case examination of the relevant facts, which has resulted in a complex web of laws, rulings, and jurisprudence that is difficult for almost anyone to fully comprehend. Nonetheless, all the legal nuance surrounding police interactions relies on the foundation built by the Constitution, and possessing a basic understanding of how this document relates to modern police encounters can dramatically improve your ability to navigate a police encounter of your own.

The Constitution and Civilian Rights

The Constitution has been interpreted by various courts in many ways throughout the years, and although there are a litany of rulings and doctrines deciphering the complexities of each amendment, analyzing the actual language of these amendments can serve as a valuable tool for understanding your rights. The Constitution contains a total of 27 amendments covering a broad range of topics, but only six of these directly apply to everyday police interactions: the First Amendment, the Fourth Amendment, the Fifth Amendment, the Sixth Amendment, the Eighth Amendment, and the Fourteenth Amendment.

Understanding these six amendments will build a foundation of civilian rights knowledge that will not only allow you to navigate police interactions safely, but will also open the door to gaining a deeper understanding of the legal system as a whole. Each of these amendments play their own vital role in ensuring that every American in this country is treated fairly by any government agent.

The First Amendment

"Congress shall make no law respecting an establishment of religion, or prohibiting the free exercise thereof; or abridging the freedom of speech, or of the press; or the right of the people peaceably to assemble, and to petition the Government for a redress of grievances."

The First Amendment guarantees the citizens of the United States five main protections:

1. The Freedom of Religion

This freedom prohibits the government from establishing an official religion or favoring one religion over another, and also guarantees individuals the right to practice their religion freely without government interference.

2. The Freedom of Speech

This freedom protects individuals' rights to express their opinions and ideas without government censorship or restraint. It covers a wide range of expression, including spoken words, written communication, symbolic speech, and expressive acts.

3. The Freedom of the Press

This freedom ensures that the press can operate independently and report news without government control or censorship. It is essential for a functioning democracy, as it allows for the dissemination of information and holds the government accountable to its citizens.

4. The Freedom to Assemble

This freedom allows citizens to gather peacefully for demonstrations, protests, and other collective activities, and ensures that people can come together to express their views and advocate for change without government intervention.

5. The Freedom to Petition the Government

This freedom grants individuals the right to make their grievances known to the government and to request action or changes in policy. It includes the ability to gather signatures for petitions, lobby government officials, and file lawsuits.

In the context of police interactions the First Amendment protects your right to express dissent against the government or its agents, such as police officers or other public officials, as well as the right to record and document any encounters you have with them. It also protects your right to protest against the police, public officials, or for any other cause you are compelled to demonstrate for. If a member of law enforcement, or any other government official, silences your speech because they don't like what you're saying, stops you from recording a police interaction in a public place, or prevents you from filing a complaint against them, then they may have violated your First Amendment rights.

The Fourth Amendment

"The right of the people to be secure in their persons, houses, papers, and effects, against unreasonable searches and seizures, shall not be violated, and no Warrants shall issue, but upon probable cause, supported by Oath or affirmation, and particularly describing the place to be searched, and the persons or things to be seized."

The legal intricacies of the Fourth Amendment influence almost every aspect of police interactions and it may be the most crucial amendment regarding civilian rights. It serves as a cornerstone of American civil liberties and provides essential protections against unreasonable searches and seizures by the government or its agents. This amendment ensures that police officers cannot illegally search you, your personal property, your car, or any other private space without your permission. It requires that any search or seizure be reasonable and backed by a legitimate warrant or legal standard, and guarantees that citizens have a right to privacy on their own property.

As Justice Byron R. White noted in the 1967 Supreme Court case of Camara v. Municipal Court:

"The basic purpose of this Amendment, as recognized in countless decisions of this Court, is to safeguard the privacy and security of individuals against arbitrary invasions by governmental officials."

The Fourth Amendment dictates how, why, when, where, and

for how long a police officer may stop you, and understanding the rights guaranteed to you by this amendment is essential to recognizing and reacting to police misconduct. The Fourth Amendment's requirements for reasonableness, warrants, and probable cause are essential components of a fair and just legal system and reflects the Constitution's intent to safeguard liberty and prevent tyranny. We will discuss the Fourth Amendment in more detail in a later chapter, but for now it's important to know that its protections are fundamental to maintaining the balance between public safety and personal privacy.

The Fifth Amendment

"No person shall be held to answer for a capital, or otherwise infamous crime, unless on a presentment or indictment of a Grand Jury, except in cases arising in the land or naval forces, or in the Militia, when in actual service in time of War or public danger; nor shall any person be subject for the same offence to be twice put in jeopardy of life or limb; nor shall be compelled in any criminal case to be a witness against himself, nor be deprived of life, liberty, or property, without due process of law; nor shall private property be taken for public use, without just compensation."

The language of the Fifth Amendment established several different constitutional rights and covered a few different topics, but its main focus was aimed at limiting the government's powers regarding criminal procedure. The Fifth Amendment is comprised of five primary clauses that make up the body of protections it guarantees to citizens:

1. Grand Jury Clause

This clause is designed to provide a check against arbitrary prosecution by the government, and specifically requires that for any felony or otherwise "infamous" crime, a person cannot be charged unless a grand jury has reviewed the evidence and issued an indictment. A grand jury is a group of citizens selected to review evidence presented by the prosecutor to determine whether there is a case against the accused person. This process is intended to protect individuals from unfounded or politically motivated charges. The Grand Jury Clause is not particularly relevant to navigating police interactions, however, it is worth researching if you want to have a comprehensive understanding of the legal system as a whole.

2. Double Jeopardy Clause

This is one of the more infamous clauses of the Fifth Amendment, as it has been showcased in several Hollywood productions throughout the years. In fact, there is a movie titled "Double Jeopardy" from 1999, starring Tommy Lee Jones and Ashley Judd, that is based around the legal concepts of this clause. Just like in the movies, the Double Jeopardy clause protects citizens from being unfairly convicted for the same crime multiple times, but it also offers three other protections from unfair prosecution and punishment from the government: protection against prosecution after an acquittal, protection from prosecution after certain mistrials, and protection from multiple punishments for the same crime. Much like the Grand Jury Clause, the Double Jeopardy clause generally does not apply to police interactions, but it is an interesting legal concept that can offer valuable insights into the world of law.

3. Self-Incrimination Clause

If you've ever heard the phrase "You have the right to remain silent," or "I plead the Fifth," then you're probably at least somewhat familiar with the Self-Incrimination Clause. This clause is an extremely valuable asset to the civil liberties guaranteed by the Constitution and is deeply woven into the fabric of every police interaction.

At its core, the Self-Incrimination Clause ensures that citizens have the right to remain silent when faced with questions or demands for information that could lead to their own prosecution. This protection applies during police interrogations, trials, and other legal processes. By invoking their right against self-incrimination, individuals can refuse to answer questions or provide statements that might be used as evidence of their guilt. This clause embodies a fundamental principle of justice: the burden of proof lies with the prosecution, not the accused. It prevents the government from using coercive or unlawful methods to extract admissions of guilt. This safeguard is essential in maintaining the integrity of the legal system and ensuring that confessions are made voluntarily, without pressure or duress.

The Self-Incrimination Clause is also closely linked to Miranda rights, which require law enforcement officers to inform citizens of their right to remain silent and to have an attorney present during custodial interrogation. This connection further underscores the importance of protecting individuals from compelled self-incrimination and reinforces the foundational idea that the state must prove its case without relying on the forced testimony of the accused. We will discuss this clause further in a later chapter, but it should be noted that the Self-Incrimination Clause serves as a vital protection for individual liberty and the right to remain silent is an essential tool for navigating police encounters.

4. Due Process Clause

Due process is a fundamental legal principle that guarantees fair treatment to citizens during any legal proceedings or judicial processes. Similar to the Fourteenth Amendment, which we will discuss later, the Fifth Amendment has its own Due Process Clause that states that no person shall "be deprived of life, liberty, or property, without due process of law." This clause was designed to ensure that the government would respect all legal rights owed to a citizen according to the law, and guarantees that the government cannot take away a person's basic rights without following fair and established procedures. It acts as a safeguard against arbitrary and unfair actions by the government and requires that any legal proceeding be conducted in a fair and orderly manner, providing individuals with notice of the proceedings and an opportunity to be heard. This means that before depriving someone of their life, freedom, or property, the government must provide a fair and transparent process that includes appropriate legal protections for the citizen.

5. Takings Clause

Of the five clauses, the Takings Clause is considered by many to be one of the more controversial clauses of the Fifth Amendment. This clause establishes two essential principles: the government's authority to take private property for public purposes, known as eminent domain, and the requirement that property owners be fairly compensated for such takings. The clause operates on the premise that, while the government has the power to seize private property to serve public interests, such as building roads, schools, or other public infrastructure, it must do so in a manner that is fair to the property owner. "Just compensation" typically means the fair market value of the property at the time of the taking, ensuring that the owner is not financially disadvantaged by the loss of their property, however, what constitutes "fair market value" is often a point of contention in cases involving eminent domain. The intention of this clause was to establish a balance between the practical needs of society and the property rights of private individuals, but the invocation of eminent domain often results in a lengthy court battle. Although the Takings Clause does not directly apply to everyday police interactions, it still plays a major role in protecting citizens from government overreach and preserving private property rights.

The importance of the Fifth Amendment in the context of police interactions cannot be understated. It operates as a bulwark for personal freedoms and justice, providing protections against arbitrary legal actions, ensuring fair procedures, and upholding individual rights in the face of governmental authority. Understanding and applying the rights guaranteed by the Fifth Amendment will have a profound effect on the outcome of your own police encounters and any legal battles that may arise afterwards.

While the First, Fourth, and Fifth Amendments typically apply directly to police interactions before or as they take place, the Sixth, Eighth, and Fourteenth Amendments generally apply after an arrest has been made. These amendments outline the procedural process that must be followed once you are in the custody of the government and your rights during that time.

The Sixth Amendment

"In all criminal prosecutions, the accused shall enjoy the right to a speedy and public trial, by an impartial jury of the State and district wherein the crime shall have been committed, which district shall have been previously ascertained by law, and to be informed of the nature and cause of the accusation; to be confronted with the witnesses against him; to have compulsory process for obtaining witnesses in his favor, and to have the Assistance of Counsel for his defence."

The protections of the Sixth Amendment begin the moment you are taken into custody, and influence how police and prosecutors must conduct themselves throughout the legal process. This amendment laid the foundation for how the modern court system works and is instrumental for properly navigating an arrest and the subsequent aftermath of an arrest. It affirms that anyone facing criminal prosecution is guaranteed a fair legal process by mandating several key rights which collectively aim to maintain the integrity of the legal system and protect citizens from potential abuses of power by the government.

The primary focus of the Sixth Amendment is to guarantee citizens the right to a transparent, speedy and public trial, and ensure that citizens are not subjected to prolonged detention without facing formal charges. This also ensures that legal proceedings are open to public scrutiny, which discourages corruption. By conducting trials openly, the justice system is held to higher standards of fairness, helping to prevent unfair or biased proceedings.

Another critical provision is the right to an impartial jury. All Americans are entitled to a trial by a jury of their peers if they are tried for a criminal offense, but the Sixth Amendment also guarantees that the jury be made up of unbiased peers that are drawn from the relevant community. The jury must be representative of the public and draw upon a fair assessment of the evidence rather than preconceived notions or external influences.

The Sixth Amendment also stipulates that the accused must be informed of the nature and cause of the accusations against them. This ensures that individuals have enough time and information available to them to prepare a legitimate defense to any charges they may be facing, and prevents the prosecution from surprising the defense with undisclosed allegations.

The right to confront witnesses is another vital provision of the Sixth Amendment, but it is also often misunderstood. This confrontation clause grants citizens accused of a crime the ability to cross-examine all witnesses who testify against them. It is important to note that this only applies to the legal proceedings after an arrest has been made. If you are being arrested based on allegations laid against you by a third party, you are not entitled to face your accuser until you appear in court.

The right to obtain your own witnesses is also guaranteed by the Sixth Amendment, which allows citizens to summon witnesses who can provide supportive evidence so that the defense can present a comprehensive and robust case.

The Sixth Amendment's guarantee for the right to legal

counsel is the most well-known aspect of the amendment in the context of police interactions. This clause provides citizens the right to legal representation throughout the criminal process, regardless of whether or not they can afford to hire their own. It is important to bear in mind that this clause does not go into effect until after an arrest has taken place. You are not entitled to legal representation in the midst of an arrest, and the right to speak to an attorney is reserved for the legal proceedings following an arrest, not as you are being detained or handcuffed.

The legal proceedings following any police interaction are equally as important as the encounter itself, and the Sixth Amendment establishes a framework that is designed to promote fairness, transparency, and justice in criminal prosecutions. Understanding how and when to utilize the protections of the Sixth Amendment can help to navigate police interactions with the foresight of what comes next after the interaction has concluded.

The Eighth Amendment

"Excessive bail shall not be required, nor excessive fines imposed, nor cruel and unusual punishments inflicted."

Considering the brevity of the Eighth Amendment, it can largely be taken at face value, however, it does warrant a brief explanation.

When a citizen is arrested, the Eighth Amendment's prohibition against excessive bail comes into play. After an arrest, a judge will typically set bail, which is an amount of money that the arrested citizen must pay to be released from custody while awaiting trial. The Eighth Amendment ensures that this bail amount is not set excessively high, which would effectively deny the individual their freedom before being convicted of a crime. The bail amount is typically proportionate to the severity of the alleged offense, but other factors, such as the citizen's ability to flee the country, may be considered.

In addition to bail, the Eighth Amendment protects individuals from excessive fines. Just like with bail, the amount of money that must be paid as a fine has to be proportionate to the severity of the crime that was committed.

The Eighth Amendment's prohibition against cruel and unusual punishments is another relevant clause of the amendment in the context of post-arrest constitutional rights. This clause ensures that individuals are not subjected to inhumane treatment or excessive force after their conviction, and has been central to debates and cases involving the death penalty, prison conditions, excessive bail, and the length of prison sentences. Any use of excessive force that causes unnecessary harm or suffering to an inmate could potentially be considered a violation of the Eighth Amendment.

Violations of the Eighth Amendment come in many forms and can range from life-altering excessive force by police officers to unsanitary jail conditions, and these protections guarantee citizens are treated fairly and humanely throughout their interactions with the criminal justice system.

The Fourteenth Amendment

Unlike the previous amendments, the Fourteenth Amendment is not a part of the Bill of Rights, and was added much later in the history of the Constitution. The primary focus of the amendment was to address citizenship rights and equal protection under the law, and it was proposed in response to issues related to formerly enslaved Americans following the Civil War. Although the amendment was subjected to political attacks, it was ultimately added to the Constitution in 1868.

The Fourteenth Amendment is divided into five distinct sections that each address citizenship rights and equal protections under the law, but only the first section applies to police interactions. It reads:

"All persons born or naturalized in the United States, and subject to the jurisdiction thereof, are citizens of the United States and of the State wherein they reside. No State shall make or enforce any law which shall abridge the privileges or immunities of citizens of the United States; nor shall any State deprive any person of life, liberty, or property, without due process of law; nor deny to any person within its jurisdiction the equal protection of the laws."

Section One of the Fourteenth Amendment is one of the most litigated parts of the Constitution, forming the basis for landmark Supreme Court decisions regarding all manner of cases involving free speech, protest, interracial marriage, and a host of other topics. This section established that all persons born or naturalized in the United States are citizens of the country and the state where they reside, and that all citizens, regardless of their background, are entitled to the same legal protections.

The Fourteenth Amendment also bars states from enforcing any laws that "deny to any person within its jurisdiction the equal protection of the laws," which is known as the 'Equal Protection Clause.' This means that law enforcement officers must apply the law impartially and without discrimination, and practices such as racial profiling or biased policing are violations of this clause because they deny individuals equal treatment under the law based on their race, ethnicity, or other protected characteristics.

The Equal Protection Clause is a crucial mechanism for holding members of law enforcement accountable, particularly for challenging discriminatory police practices. If certain racial or ethnic groups are disproportionately targeted by law enforcement, these practices can be contested as unconstitutional under this clause. The amendment's requirement for equal treatment under the law acts as a check against systemic biases in policing.

The section goes on to state that no person shall be deprived of life, liberty, or property without due process of law. This is known as the 'Due Process Clause' of the Fourteenth Amendment. Although this clause doesn't apply to everyday police interactions in a direct way, it is still a vital safeguard that preserves fairness in legal procedures and protects certain fundamental rights. The Due Process Clause shapes much of the legal landscape surrounding constitutional law, and guarantees that citizens are treated fairly by the judicial system.

The First, Fourth, Fifth, Sixth, Eighth, and Fourteenth Amendments collectively provide a comprehensive framework of protections that guide and constrain police interactions, preserving justice, fairness, and respect for constitutional rights. Understanding the protections guaranteed by these amendments will allow you to recognize when police misconduct is taking place and what to do once misconduct has occurred. This awareness empowers you to respond appropriately to any unlawful or unfair treatment and allows you to make informed decisions that can significantly impact the outcome of an interaction. However, the practical application of these rights often depends on how they are interpreted and enforced by the courts.

One of the many roles of our judicial system is to interpret the language of the Constitution and apply it to modern cases. Courts define the scope and limits of constitutional protections and make critical decisions that shape the relationship between law enforcement authority and civilian rights. Understanding what constitutional protections are available to you is only half the puzzle. You should also understand how those rights have been interpreted and applied by higher courts, and how the judicial system operates as a whole. Once you have a thorough understanding of both the Constitution and the court's interpretation of it, you can rest assured that you're prepared to handle almost any police encounter.

Courts and the Judicial System

The American Federal judicial system operates as a structured hierarchy designed to interpret and apply the law consistently across the country and ensure that laws, and the legal process itself, operate in a manner that is consistent with the Constitution. This system has played a crucial role in shaping modern police interactions, and understanding how this system works is just as important as understanding the Constitution.

Although the Constitution is the supreme law of the land, each state also has its own constitution and its own court system tasked with interpreting and applying its respective laws. These courts handle a wide range of cases, from minor offenses to serious felonies, and serve as the primary venues for fact-finding and initial legal determinations. Judges and juries in these courts listen to evidence, witness testimonies, and legal arguments, and make decisions based on state laws.

If you are charged with a crime, an appearance at your local court will likely be your first opportunity to present evidence supporting your innocence, plead guilty, or make a deal with the prosecutor.

When legal errors or disputes arise, cases can be appealed to the state appellate courts, which review trial court proceedings to ensure the correct application of law. These intermediate courts do not conduct new trials but evaluate the trial record and legal briefs to determine if errors occurred that warrant reversing or modifying the lower court's decision.

If you are found guilty of a crime you will have an opportunity to appeal the findings of the state court and ask for a review of your case from an appellate court. The appellate court may disagree with the state court's ruling and reverse their decision, it may uphold the state court's decision, or in some situations, it may refuse to hear your case altogether.

At the pinnacle of the state judicial system are the state supreme courts. What these courts are called can vary between states. While some states have a 'Supreme Court,' others might have a 'Court of Appeals.' These courts hold the ultimate authority within each state, resolving conflicts in legal interpretation and ensuring fairness and uniformity in the application of state law. They select cases that present significant legal questions or require resolution of discrepancies between lower court rulings. Decisions made by state supreme courts set binding precedents for all other courts in the state, and guide future judicial decisions and law enforcement practices. Nonetheless, even state supreme courts are beholden to the rulings of the federal Supreme Court.

If you disagree with the ruling of the appellate court you will have the opportunity to appeal your case to the state supreme court, however, the odds of having your case selected for review are very low if they don't involve some sort of unique legal concept or dispute. If your case is selected by a state's supreme court, and they rule against you, you can appeal your case even further to the U.S. Supreme Court. The odds of having your case selected for review by this court are even more slim.

Parallel to the state courts is the federal judiciary, beginning with the district courts. These courts serve as the trial courts for federal cases, addressing issues involving federal laws, civil rights, and criminal offenses that cross state lines. District courts handle the bulk of federal litigation, conducting trials where judges or juries determine the facts and apply federal statutes. Decisions from these courts can be appealed to the United States court of appeals, which reviews the application of law in district court cases. The court of appeals is commonly referred to as the "Circuit Court" because the country is divided into 12 regional circuits, each overseeing cases within specific geographic areas.

These appellate courts examine trial records and legal arguments from across their region to uphold or reverse lower court decisions. However, the rulings issued by the various circuits are not always consistent with each other. For example, the Fifth Circuit Court of Appeals, which has jurisdiction over Texas, Louisiana, and Mississippi, may rule differently on a particular law or legal concept than the Eleventh Circuit Court of Appeals, which has jurisdiction over Alabama, Florida, and Georgia. This is commonly referred to as a "circuit split." In other words, the rulings of these courts can result in different laws and legal standards in different circuits, and some jurisdictions may have laws that are less favorable to civilian rights than others.

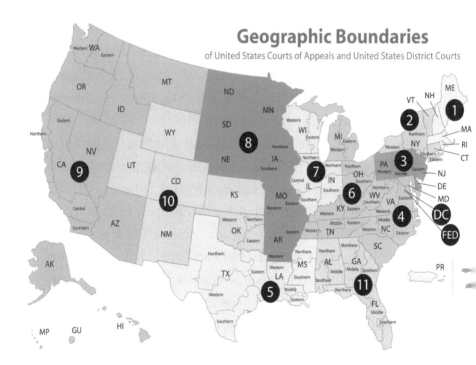

Geographic Boundaries
of United States Courts of Appeals and United States District Courts

For example: In the 2007 case of United States v. Garcia the Seventh Circuit Court of Appeals ruled that attaching a GPS device to a citizen's vehicle to track their movements without a warrant was not a violation of the Fourth Amendment, however, in 2012 the United States Court of Appeals for the District of Columbia Circuit reached the opposite conclusion and ruled that the warrantless use of a GPS device was a violation of a citizen's reasonable expectation of privacy granted by the Fourth Amendment. At the time, these rulings sparked significant legal debate and prompted the Supreme Court to take on the case and eventually rule that using a GPS device to track a person without their consent or a valid warrant is a violation of the Fourth Amendment.

At the apex of the American judicial system, the Supreme Court of the United States is the highest court in the nation. It is made up of nine highly qualified legal experts known as "justices" who are appointed for life. This Court has the authority to review cases from both federal and state courts, primarily focusing on issues of constitutional significance. The Court selects a very limited number of cases and requires agreement from at least four justices to hear a case.

The Supreme Court's interpretations of the Constitution set standards for all other courts to follow, which has a profound effect on the law, civilian rights, and police interactions as a whole. When the Supreme Court issues a ruling, it must be adhered to by every court in the entire country. The Court's primary objective is to determine whether the rulings of lower courts abide by the language, standards, and intentions of the Constitution.

U.S. Supreme Court

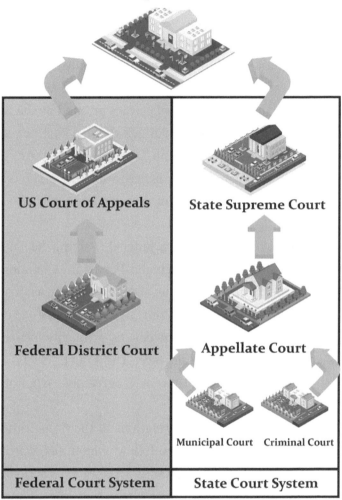

* State court systems can vary, but this illustrates the basic judicial framework.

To gain a better understanding of how the judicial system works on a practical level, let's take a look at a case that made it to the Supreme Court, and examine the process and legal disputes that led it to the highest court in the land.

In 1965, a California man named Charles Katz had built a reputation for being a proficient sports bettor. He would regularly use the public phone booth just outside his apartment building in Los Angeles to place bets with bookies in other states, which is illegal under Section 18 of the United States Code. Eventually the FBI became interested in Katz's gambling activities and attached a covert listening device to the outside of the phone booth. After spying on several of Katz's phone calls, the FBI arrested him and charged him with eight counts of knowingly transmitting wagering information by telephone between U.S. states.

The case was first tried in the U.S. District Court for the Southern District of California, which is the lowest level federal court. Katz's attorneys argued that the recordings should not be admissible in court because they violated his Fourth Amendment rights. The FBI did not have a warrant to place the listening device, and telephone booths are considered a space where citizens are entitled to a reasonable expectation of privacy. The District Court disagreed with Katz's lawyers and he was convicted based on evidence provided by the recordings.

Katz appealed the District Court's ruling to the Ninth Circuit Court of Appeals, which has jurisdiction over California and many other western states and territories. The Circuit Court agreed to review the case, but affirmed the decision of the District Court and upheld Katz's conviction. The Circuit Court reasoned that because the FBI's listening device did not physically penetrate the wall of the telephone booth, no search occurred, and so the FBI did not need a warrant to place the device or record the conversations.

At this point a relatively dangerous precedent had been set

that would allow federal agents and police officers to record private conversations so long as they did not physically enter a private space. A ruling like this would effectively make no place truly private if it is accessible by a powerful enough listening device. Katz's legal team had no choice but to appeal his case to the Supreme Court and hope that the justices would recognize the alarming implications of the previous courts' rulings.

The Supreme Court quickly took on the case and reversed the rulings of the previous two courts, overturning Katz's conviction and ruling that the FBI's use of a listening device violated Katz's Fourth Amendment protections. The Court concluded that Katz was entitled to privacy inside the phone booth, and that the Fourth Amendment required the FBI to obtain a warrant before spying on his private conversations.

The Supreme Court's decision in the Katz case derailed a legal precedent that could have had potentially devastating effects on the protections of the Fourth Amendment, and established a more expansive interpretation of privacy rights that guarantees individuals are protected against unwarranted government surveillance.

The Katz case showcases the hierarchical nature of the American judicial system and demonstrates how the appeal process works. State judicial systems employ similarly hierarchical structures, and are also ultimately beholden to the rulings of the U.S. Supreme Court.

The Constitution and the Judicial System are both fundamental elements of the concept of civilian rights as a whole, and gaining an understanding of how they function is the first step to becoming an informed citizen. Throughout this book, we will refer to the Constitution and various court rulings. With this context in mind, we can now explore how they apply to police interactions in everyday life.

Chapter Two
The Foundation of Freedom

Imagine walking down a quiet street at dusk, the glow of streetlights casting long shadows. A police car slows beside you, and an officer steps out, approaching with purposeful strides. At that moment, a myriad of questions might flood your mind: Do I have to answer their questions? Can they search my belongings? What are my rights? In this chapter we will explore how the Fourth Amendment applies to everyday police interactions on a practical level, and dive into the concepts of search and seizure.

The Fourth Amendment is a fundamental component of the Bill of Rights that safeguards citizens' privacy and personal security against unreasonable government intrusion. This amendment provides critical protections during interactions with law enforcement, shaping how police conduct searches, seizures, and arrests. For citizens, the Fourth Amendment means that they have the right to be secure in their persons and properties. During police interactions, this amendment often comes into play when an officer stops an individual, conducts a search, or makes an arrest.

The Fourth Amendment also implies that citizens have the right to question the legality of police actions. If a citizen believes that they have been subjected to an unreasonable search or seizure, they have the right to challenge the validity of the police conduct in court. The Fourth Amendment serves as the cornerstone for the preservation of civil liberties, and plays a role in nearly every police interaction that takes place. By being aware of these protections, citizens can navigate interactions with law enforcement more confidently, safeguarding their privacy and personal security against unwarranted intrusions.

Search and Seizure

Anytime the police search a citizen's car, home, private property, or the citizen themselves, the Fourth Amendment is implicated, and citizens are entitled to certain protections from unreasonable searches. Whether an officer is within their authority to conduct a search is highly dependent on several different factors, such as the circumstances surrounding the search, the conduct of the officers involved, and whether or not the officers had a warrant.

The modern view of searches in the context of police interactions under the Fourth Amendment is shaped by several landmark Supreme Court cases and legal doctrines that establish the boundaries of what constitutes a reasonable search and ensure that law enforcement actions are balanced against individual rights. The same can be said for seizures. Anytime the police take property that doesn't belong to them, it is considered a seizure, and the protections of the Fourth Amendment are implicated.

Whenever a police officer stops a citizen, the principles of search and seizure dictate the boundaries of that encounter and operate as a legal framework for transforming abstract constitutional promises into tangible protections for individuals. Every police interaction, every stop, every search, is a real-world application of these doctrines, constantly tested and refined through the judicial process. Understanding these principles empowers citizens. It provides a lens through which to view police encounters, to recognize when rights might be infringed upon, and to seek accountability.

At the heart of the Fourth Amendment lies a fundamental promise:

"The right of the people to be secure in their persons, houses, papers, and effects, against unreasonable searches and seizures, shall not be violated..."

This powerful statement establishes a protective barrier between citizens and the government's potential overreach. But what does it mean in practical terms? To fully grasp its implications, we must dissect the concepts of "search" and "seizure" and understand how they apply in everyday situations.

Defining a Search

A "search" occurs when a government official intrudes upon an area where you have a reasonable expectation of privacy. This concept was solidified in the Katz case we discussed in chapter one, where the Supreme Court held that the Fourth Amendment protects people, not just places.

Prior to the Katz case, the courts interpreted the Fourth Amendment as only protecting against physical intrusions into a person's property. Early landmark cases like Boyd v. United States from 1886 and the 1914 case of Weeks v. United States focused on the protection of physical spaces, particularly a person's home or property, from government intrusion. Searches were typically seen as unlawful if they involved a physical entry into a protected space without a warrant.

In the Katz case, the FBI had placed a listening device on a public phone booth to eavesdrop on the defendant's conversations. The Court ruled that the defendant had a "reasonable expectation of privacy" in the phone booth, rendering the government's actions a "search" under the Fourth Amendment.

Along with redefining the concept of a search, the Katz case was the first to acknowledge that the "reasonable expectation of privacy" was a critical element to be considered when determining whether a search had occurred. Although Justice Stewart wrote the opinion of the Court, it was Justice John Marshall Harlan II's concurring opinion that became the most influential part of the case. Harlan introduced the now-famous "reasonable expectation of privacy" test, which has since become the standard for determining whether a Fourth Amendment violation has occurred.

The "reasonable expectation of privacy" test is twofold and considers the following:

1. Subjective Expectation of Privacy: Did the individual exhibit an actual, subjective expectation of privacy in the thing or place being searched?

2. Objective Expectation of Privacy: Is the individual's expectation of privacy one that society is prepared to recognize as reasonable?

In the Katz case, the defendant closed the door behind him as he entered the bugged phone booth, which suggested to the court that he "subjectively" expected privacy while conducting his conversation. This satisfied the first prong of Justice Harlan's test. The Katz Court went on to explain that phone booths were generally understood to offer privacy for telephone conversations, meaning that Mr. Katz also had an "objective" expectation of privacy that had been acknowledged by the public at large, thereby satisfying the second prong of the test.

The establishment of Justice Harlan's test shifted the focus of the Fourth Amendment away from purely physical locations and in favor of an approach that protects individual citizens as well. The following quote from the Katz case encapsulates the Court's reasoning for shifting the legal precedent of searches:

"For the Fourth Amendment protects people, not places. What a person knowingly exposes to the public, even in his own home or office, is not a subject of Fourth Amendment protection. But what he seeks to preserve as private, even in an area accessible to the public, may be constitutionally protected."

In other words, the protections guaranteed by the Fourth Amendment cannot be neatly reduced to whether or not private property is involved, and there are some circumstances where citizens are entitled to Fourth Amendment protections while in public. Citizens are entitled to privacy if their expectation of privacy is reasonable given the circumstances, and this is the basis from which a court will determine whether or not a search was lawful.

The difference between subjective and objective expectations of privacy is central to Fourth Amendment analysis. A person must first subjectively expect privacy, but that expectation must also be deemed reasonable by societal standards for Fourth Amendment protections to apply.

For example, when a person closes the blinds in their home, they are exhibiting a subjective expectation that their activities inside the home are private and shielded from public view. Courts have long recognized that individuals have a reasonable, objective expectation of privacy inside their homes. This means that being inside of your home with the windows covered establishes both a subjective and objective expectation of privacy, making it extremely difficult to justify a warrantless entry or search.

Similarly, an individual who enters a stall in a public restroom and locks the door likely assumes their activities inside are private, establishing a subjective expectation of privacy. And because society generally agrees that privacy is expected in such intimate settings, courts typically recognize an objective expectation of privacy in a closed bathroom stall.

The reasonable expectation of privacy establishes the boundary between what individuals are entitled to keep private and when the government can intrude on that privacy. If an individual has a reasonable expectation of privacy, members of law enforcement generally need a warrant to conduct a search.

Therefore, a "search" can be defined as any act perpetrated by government agents that disrupts or intrudes upon a person's property or their reasonable expectation of privacy, regardless of the setting.

Defining a Seizure

In the context of police interactions, a "seizure" can apply to both individuals and their property. A seizure of property occurs when the government interferes with an individual's possession or access to their own property, and a seizure of a person happens whenever the government interferes with a person's freedom of movement.

Before we discuss the intricacies of what constitutes a seizure by the police, it is important to discuss encounters with the police that are not considered a seizure, otherwise known as "consensual encounters." Consensual encounters occur on the basis of consent, meaning that you are giving your consent for the encounter to take place and you may revoke that consent at any time and walk away. A consensual encounter occurs when police officers approach an individual and engage in conversation without exerting any coercive pressure or authority. The hallmark of a consensual encounter is the voluntary nature of the interaction. For instance, if an officer approaches someone on the street to ask if they have seen anything suspicious in the area, and the individual chooses to engage in the conversation, this would be considered a consensual encounter.

Since there is no restraint on the individual's freedom to walk away, this type of encounter does not require any suspicion of criminal activity and does not invoke the Fourth Amendment protections against unreasonable searches and seizures. On the contrary, if the individual were to reject the officer's questioning, but the officer insisted that they stay and be questioned, this would be considered a 'nonconsensual encounter.' Nonconsensual encounters occur when an individual is not free to leave an interaction with the police and is lawfully compelled to follow their orders. All nonconsensual encounters with members of law enforcement are considered "seizures" under the Fourth Amendment.

The distinction between consensual and nonconsensual encounters was decided in the 1980 Supreme Court case of United States v. Mendenhall, where the Court established a legal precedent designed to determine whether an interaction with the police was consensual or not known as the "Mendenhall Test." At the core of the Mendenhall Test is the following quote from the Court:

"We conclude that a person has been "seized" within the meaning of the Fourth Amendment only if, in view of all of the circumstances surrounding the incident, a reasonable person would have believed that he was not free to leave."

This means that if police officers engage in activity that would make the average person feel as though they were not free to leave at any time, then the encounter would be considered nonconsensual, and thus, a seizure. Any show of authority or use of force that is intended to compel a citizen to interact with an officer renders the encounter nonconsensual. While this may seem relatively straightforward when taken at face value, the distinction between a consensual encounter and a nonconsensual encounter can be difficult to recognize during a police interaction. The Mendenhall Court went on to provide four examples of circumstances that might indicate a nonconsensual encounter is taking place:

1. The threatening presence of several officers

The presence of multiple officers can create a coercive atmosphere that significantly impacts an individual's perception of their freedom to leave. Multiple officers can appear intimidating, and can imply a potential use of force if the individual attempts to leave or does not comply with their requests.

2. The display of a weapon by an officer

Using or handling a weapon in a manner that is intended to force compliance renders the encounter nonconsensual. When officers display their weapons, even if they are not explicitly threatening to use them, it can suggest to the individual that force may be used if they do not comply. This creates a coercive environment where the citizen feels compelled to obey.

3. Some physical touching of the citizen

When an officer physically touches an individual, it can be seen as an immediate assertion of authority. This act signals that the officer is in control of the situation and that the individual is not free to move or leave. Even minor physical contact, such as placing a hand on someone's shoulder or arm, can convey this message.

4. The use of language indicating that compliance is lawfully required

When officers use authoritative or commanding language, it can imply that they are exercising their official power and that the individual must comply with their requests. Phrases like "You need to stay here," "I need to see your ID," or "You must answer my questions" can suggest that compliance is not optional, even if the officer does not explicitly say so. Even a harsh, stern, or aggressive tone of voice can be considered intimidation.

Interactions with the police often begin as consensual encounters but eventually evolve into nonconsensual encounters, and this can happen either very quickly or slowly and subtly. Although the Supreme Court laid out clear cut rules for consensual and nonconsensual encounters in the Mendenhall case, how and when these rules go into effect can be difficult to detect during a police interaction.

It is important to note that you are not actually seized until you physically submit to the authority of the officer. In the 1991 Supreme Court case of California v. Hodari D, the Court clarified that a seizure requires either physical force or submission to the authority of an officer. In other words, this means that if an officer tells you to stop and you keep walking, you aren't legally 'seized' until you either stop or the officer physically stops you.

Along with protecting the seizure of people, the Fourth Amendment also offers protections against the unlawful seizure of property. At its core, a "seizure" of property occurs when government action meaningfully interferes with an individual's possessory interests in that property. This definition was articulated in the landmark 1984 case of United States v. Jacobsen, where the Supreme Court clarified that a seizure of property occurs when there is some meaningful interference with an individual's possessory interests in that property. In other words, whenever the government takes or blocks access to your property, they are effectively "seizing" it, however, there are certain exceptions and intricacies that apply to property seizures.

In the Jacobsen case, Federal Express employees had opened

a damaged package and found white powder inside, which they suspected was illegal drugs. They notified the DEA, and agents conducted a field test on the substance without a warrant. The Court held that the field test was not a violation of the Fourth Amendment because it did not compromise any legitimate interest in privacy or meaningfully interfere with possessory interests beyond what the private parties had already done. Testing the powder could only possibly reveal whether or not the substance was illegal drugs, which does not have a privacy right. If the test results were negative for illegal drugs, then the individuals conducting the test would know nothing more about the substance than they did before they administered the test, beyond the fact that the substance was not illegal drugs. The key takeaway is that not every interaction with property constitutes a seizure; the interference must be significant enough to impact the owner's control or use of the property.

The notion of "meaningful interference" is crucial as it differentiates trivial or incidental contact with property from actions that legally amount to a seizure. For instance, if a police officer briefly picks up an item to examine it without removing it from the owner's presence or impeding its use, this may not constitute a seizure. However, if the officer takes possession of the item or restricts the owner's access to it, this would likely be considered a seizure under the Fourth Amendment.

We will discuss the practical application of the concepts of search and seizure in a later chapter, but it is important to understand that when exactly a seizure of people or property takes place is often difficult to discern and largely subject to the ruling of a court on a case-by-case basis. If you are ever in a situation where you believe you are being unlawfully searched or having your property unlawfully seized, it is almost always in your best interest to comply with the search or seizure and file a lawsuit afterwards.

The Warrant Requirement

One of the fundamental elements of the Fourth Amendment is "The right of the people to be secure in their persons, houses, papers, and effects, against unreasonable searches and seizures, shall not be violated." What this has been interpreted to mean is that a warrant is required to conduct a search or seizure unless a warrant exception exists. We will discuss the concept of probable cause in the next chapter, but it is important to highlight the role that warrants play in the context of search and seizure.

A warrant is a legal document issued by a judge or magistrate, authorizing law enforcement to conduct a search, seizure, or arrest. It must be based on probable cause and must particularly describe the place to be searched and the persons or property to be seized. As described in the Fourth Amendment itself, a warrant must be very specific about what it authorizes members of law enforcement to do, and warrants that are not highly specific are generally considered to be unlawful.

The requirement for a warrant is deeply rooted in the history of the United States. The Founding Fathers were acutely aware of the abuses of general warrants and writs of assistance by British authorities, which allowed them to search homes and businesses without cause. The purpose of a warrant is to ensure that the actions of law enforcement while conducting a search or seizure are lawful. It essentially functions as the government's 'stamp of approval' for a search or seizure carried out by the police and is typically authorized by judges or magistrates that are local to the search or seizure.

Before a warrant is issued, law enforcement officers must present evidence to a judge or magistrate that establishes probable cause. This process is supposed to ensure that an independent authority, separate from law enforcement, evaluates the evidence to determine if there is enough justification to proceed with the search or seizure. The requirement that warrants be issued by a neutral magistrate was designed to act as a safeguard to prevent abuses of power by requiring an impartial third party to verify the necessity of the search or seizure.

While warrants are a key safeguard, there are situations when the police can conduct a search without one, such as if they believe evidence might be destroyed or if the suspect consents to the search. Courts have recognized several exceptions to the warrant requirement, each with specific criteria that allow officers to act swiftly while remaining within the bounds of their authority.

Exceptions to the Warrant Requirement

1. Search Incident to Lawful Arrest

The search incident to lawful arrest is one of the most well established exceptions to the warrant requirement, allowing officers to search an individual and the immediate area around them after making an arrest. The main purpose of this search is to ensure officer safety and to prevent the destruction of evidence. If a person is being arrested, it stands to reason that officers need to ensure there are no weapons within their reach that could pose a danger, or any evidence that could be quickly hidden or destroyed. These types of searches are limited to the area within the immediate reach of the arrestee, and have a fairly limited scope.

In the 1969 Supreme Court case of Chimel v. California the Court set clear limits on how far a search incident to arrest can go. When officers arrested Chimel inside his home, they proceeded to search the entire house, including drawers and other areas far beyond Chimel's reach. The Court ruled that such an extensive search was unlawful. The permissible scope of a search incident to arrest includes only the person being arrested and the immediate area from which they could potentially grab a weapon or destroy evidence, such as a nearby table or a bag within reach.

This exception also applies to searches of vehicles where a recent occupant was arrested, with certain limitations. In the 2009 Supreme Court case of Arizona v. Gant, the court held that "circumstances unique to the automobile context justify a search incident to arrest when it is reasonable to believe that evidence of the offense of arrest might be found in the vehicle." In other words, officers may search a vehicle after making an arrest if they believe the vehicle contains evidence related to the arrest. The Court in the Gant case went on to clarify that the authority to search a vehicle incident to an arrest also applies anytime the arrestee is within reaching distance of the passenger compartment, stating "Police may search a vehicle incident to a recent occupant's arrest only if the arrestee is within reaching distance of the passenger compartment at the time of the search or it is reasonable to believe the vehicle contains evidence of the offense of arrest."

Practical Example: A police officer arrests a suspect for robbery and handcuffs them. During the arrest, the officer can search the suspect's pockets for any weapons or stolen goods. Additionally, if the arrest takes place near the suspect's backpack, the officer may also search the backpack to ensure it does not contain any weapons or stolen items that could be relevant to the crime. However, the officer cannot proceed to search the suspect's entire home without a warrant, as that would exceed the immediate area of control.

2. Consent Searches

A consent search occurs whenever a citizen voluntarily gives police officers their permission to search. Consent searches can be a powerful tool for law enforcement because they do not require a warrant or even probable cause. If an individual agrees to a search, the officer can proceed. It is important to note that police officers are not required to inform citizens that they have a right to refuse consent to search, and this was confirmed by the Supreme Court in the 1973 case of Schneckloth v. Bustamonte.

In the 1991 case of Florida v. Jimeno the Court further clarified that when a person gives general consent to search their vehicle, that consent generally extends to any containers within the vehicle, provided it is reasonable to assume the consent covered them. If the officer reasonably believes that searching a closed bag is within the scope of the consent given, they may proceed without a warrant.

However, the key element of this type of warrant exception is that consent must be given freely, without any form of coercion or duress. For a consent search to be valid under the Fourth Amendment, the consent must be given voluntarily. This means that an individual must feel free to refuse the officer's request without facing undue pressure. If officers use threats, intimidation, or an abuse of authority to obtain consent, the search may be deemed unlawful.

The courts assess the voluntariness of consent by examining the "totality of the circumstances," including factors such as the individual's state of mind, the officer's behavior, and the environment in which the request was made. For example, in the 1968 case of Bumper v. North Carolina, the Supreme Court found that a search was invalid because it was obtained under duress. In this case, officers claimed they had a warrant when they did not, and the homeowner then "consented" to the search. The Court ruled that this consent was not truly voluntary because it was coerced by the officers' false statement. The ruling emphasized that when officers falsely claim legal authority, any consent given afterward cannot be considered free and voluntary, but instead was coerced through misrepresentation. Coercion can come in many forms, but the general rule of thumb is that a person must always feel that they can say "no" without repercussion for the consent to be legally valid.

Practical Example: A police officer pulls over a driver for speeding and then asks if they can search the vehicle. The driver, wanting to avoid further trouble, agrees to the search. During the search, the officer finds illegal drugs hidden under the seat. Since the driver consented, the officer did not need a warrant, and the search was lawful.

3. Exigent Circumstances

The exigent circumstances exception involves situations that demand immediate action, making it impractical for officers to obtain a warrant. These situations include scenarios where there is a risk of imminent danger, the potential destruction of evidence, or the likelihood of a suspect fleeing. Courts have upheld that the immediate nature of the threat justifies bypassing the warrant requirement. The foundation of this exception is the immediacy of the threat or need, and courts evaluate each situation based on the reasonableness of the officer's actions under the given circumstances.

Under the exigent circumstances exception officers are granted considerable authority to circumvent the Fourth Amendment during emergency situations. The severity of the suspected crime plays a major role in determining whether exigent circumstances exist. Exigent circumstances are more likely to be found when serious crimes are involved, particularly those involving violence or a threat to public safety.

For example, an officer who is pursuing a citizen suspected of a mass shooting would have much greater authority to do what is necessary to apprehend the suspect than if the suspect was wanted for a minor violation, like graffiti or jaywalking. That being said, courts consider various factors to evaluate the reasonableness of the officers' actions under the exigent circumstances exception. There are three primary types of exigent circumstances recognized by the courts:

Preventing Physical Harm or Danger to Officers or Others: This applies when officers have a reasonable belief that someone inside a residence or location is in danger or needs assistance. For example, if police hear screaming from inside a home and believe someone is being harmed, they may enter without a warrant to protect that person. In the 2006 case of Brigham City v. Stuart the Supreme Court upheld a warrantless entry where officers arrived at a house in response to a noise complaint and witnessed through a window an altercation in which a juvenile appeared to be in physical danger. The officers entered the house without a warrant to prevent harm. The Court noted that the officers had a reasonable basis to believe that immediate intervention was necessary to prevent serious injury, which qualifies as an exigent circumstance exception to the Fourth Amendment's warrant requirement. This also applies to non-crime related emergencies such as fires, gas leaks, and medical emergencies.

Preventing the Destruction of Evidence: When officers have probable cause to believe that there is evidence present, they can act immediately to preserve that evidence. This often arises in drug cases, where flushing substances down a toilet or other methods of destruction can happen rapidly. In the 2011 Supreme Court case of Kentucky v. King, police officers were in pursuit of a suspect who they believed had entered an apartment. When the officers approached, they heard noises inside that they interpreted as the destruction of evidence. They immediately entered the apartment without a warrant. The Supreme Court upheld this action, reasoning that exigent circumstances justified the warrantless entry. The Court ruled that as long as officers did not create the exigency by violating the Fourth Amendment, they could rely on the exigent circumstances to act quickly.

Hot Pursuit of a Fleeing Suspect: When officers are in active pursuit of a suspect who has committed a serious crime, they may follow that suspect into a private space, such as a home, without a warrant. The suspect's attempt to flee justifies the immediate action. A key case that outlines the "hot pursuit" exception under exigent circumstances is the 1976 Supreme Court case of United States v. Santana. In this case, police officers followed a suspect, Santana, from a public space into her home without a warrant, suspecting she was involved in drug activity. The Supreme Court ruled that the officers did not violate the Fourth Amendment by entering her home without a warrant because they were in "hot pursuit" of a felony suspect, and delaying to obtain a warrant could result in the destruction of evidence. If a citizen is suspected of committing a serious crime then the police are generally authorized to follow that suspect into their home so long as the initial interaction began lawfully.

Practical Example: Suppose officers are investigating a suspected drug dealer and have probable cause to believe that drugs are inside the residence. When they knock on the door and announce themselves, they hear rapid movement and toilets flushing. In this situation, officers may enter the home without a warrant to prevent the destruction of evidence, as waiting for a warrant could result in losing valuable evidence.

4. Automobile Exception

The automobile exception allows law enforcement officers to search a vehicle without a warrant if they have probable cause to believe that the vehicle contains evidence of a crime. This exception was established due to the unique nature of automobiles, specifically, their inherent mobility and the diminished expectation of privacy people have when they are inside vehicles compared to when they are in their homes. Courts have consistently held that requiring officers to obtain a warrant before searching a vehicle could result in the vehicle, and any evidence inside it, being moved out of reach before a warrant could be obtained.

The automobile exception is rooted in two fundamental ideas: the mobility of vehicles and the reduced expectation of privacy in vehicles. Unlike a home, which is stationary and considered a person's most protected space, a vehicle can easily be driven away, making it impractical for officers to secure the scene and obtain a warrant. Vehicles are heavily regulated by the government, including requirements for licenses, registration, and safety inspections, which contributes to lowering the expectation of privacy inside them.

The 1925 Supreme Court case of Carroll v. United States established the automobile exception, and has since set the foundation for how warrantless searches of vehicles are handled under the Fourth Amendment. In the case, federal agents had probable cause to believe that Carroll's vehicle contained illegal liquor during Prohibition. The Supreme Court ruled that the inherent mobility of vehicles justified the warrantless search, emphasizing that if officers have probable cause, they can search a vehicle immediately rather than waiting for a warrant, which could lead to the loss of evidence.

In the 1991 case of California v. Acevedo the Supreme Court expanded the automobile exception to also include containers inside the vehicle, such as a backpack or glovebox. The officers in this case witnessed Acevedo placing a paper bag into his trunk, and they had probable cause to believe that the bag contained marijuana. The Supreme Court held that officers could search not only the container but also any part of the vehicle where they had probable cause to believe evidence might be found. However, it should be noted that probable cause is required for each instance of a search, and officers cannot justify a search of an entire vehicle based on probable cause for a specific container or vice versa.

As clarified by Justice John Paul Stevens in the 1982 Supreme Court case of United States v. Ross, "Just as probable cause to believe that a stolen lawnmower may be found in a garage will not support a warrant to search an upstairs bedroom, probable cause to believe that undocumented aliens are being transported in a van will not justify a warrantless search of a suitcase. Probable cause to believe that a container placed in the trunk of a taxi contains contraband or evidence does not justify a search of the entire cab."

Once an officer establishes probable cause to believe that contraband or evidence may be found in a vehicle, they can search any part of the vehicle that could potentially contain the object of the search. This includes any container within the vehicle that is large enough to hold whatever the officer is looking for. However, if an officer only has probable cause to believe that the evidence or contraband is in a particular container placed within the vehicle, they may not search the vehicle beyond what is necessary to secure the container.

Likewise, probable cause for a search of a vehicle doesn't necessarily grant officers the authority to search every container within the vehicle. For instance, if an officer has probable cause to believe there was a stolen laptop inside a vehicle, this would not authorize the officer to search inside a wallet found inside the vehicle, as it would not be possible for the stolen laptop to be contained inside the wallet.

Under the automobile exception, police may also conduct what is known as a 'protective search' of a vehicle so long as they have reasonable suspicion and legitimately believe that weapons may be inside. In the 1983 Supreme Court case of Michigan v. Long, the Court noted that "Protection of police and others can justify protective searches when police have a reasonable belief that the suspect poses a danger. Roadside encounters between police and suspects are especially hazardous, and danger may arise from the possible presence of weapons in the area surrounding a suspect. Thus, the search of the passenger compartment of an automobile, limited to those areas in which a weapon may be placed or hidden, is permissible if the police officer possesses a reasonable belief based on specific and articulable facts which, taken together with the rational inferences from those facts, reasonably warrant the officer to believe that the suspect is dangerous and the suspect may gain immediate control of weapons." Protective searches are limited to areas where a weapon may be accessed or hidden by the suspect, but any illegal contraband that happens to be found during a protective search is still admissible in court.

The automobile exception also allows for inventory searches of vehicles that have been towed or otherwise taken into police custody, and any contraband found during these searches is also admissible in court. In the 1976 Supreme Court case of South Dakota v. Opperman the Court held that "When the police take custody of any sort of container [such as] an automobile, it is reasonable to search the container to itemize the property to be held by the police. [This reflects] the underlying principle that the fourth amendment proscribes only unreasonable searches." The Court viewed inventory searches as a matter of procedure and standard protocol, and clarified that these searches do not violate the Fourth Amendment so long as they are conducted according to standard department policy.

Practical Example: Suppose an officer pulls over a vehicle for a routine traffic violation in a state where marijuana is illegal and, during the stop, detects the odor of marijuana coming from inside the car. Based on this observation, the officer has probable cause to believe that the vehicle contains illegal drugs. Under the automobile exception, the officer can conduct a warrantless search of the vehicle, including any compartments or containers that could potentially contain the marijuana, to locate the source of the odor.

5. Plain View Doctrine

Generally, anytime an officer personally witnesses incriminating evidence during a lawful stop they are within their authority to seize that evidence without a warrant. For the plain view doctrine to apply, several conditions must be met, primarily relating to the legality of the officer's presence and the immediately apparent incriminating nature of the evidence. The plain view doctrine is designed to balance the practical needs of law enforcement with the protections guaranteed by the Fourth Amendment against unreasonable searches and seizures. The doctrine stems from the idea that, in certain situations, requiring an officer to ignore obvious evidence of a crime simply because they do not have a warrant is unreasonable and would hinder law enforcement unnecessarily. However, specific conditions must be met to ensure that the officer's observation is lawful and does not infringe upon a person's right to privacy.

The 1971 Supreme Court case of Coolidge v. New Hampshire formally established the plain view doctrine. In this case, officers seized items from Coolidge's home without a warrant, arguing that the evidence was in plain view. The Court ruled that the plain view doctrine allows for warrantless seizures only if the officer is legally present and if the evidence is immediately identifiable as incriminating. Importantly, the Court emphasized that officers must be in a place where they have the legal right to be when they make the observation.

In the 1990 case of Horton v. California the Supreme Court clarified that as long as officers are lawfully present and the evidence's incriminating nature is obvious, the seizure is lawful even if the officers expected to find such evidence. This decision made the plain view doctrine more flexible by allowing officers to seize evidence in plain view without needing it to be an accidental discovery. However, there are limitations to the plain view doctrine, and the 1987 Supreme Court case of Arizona v. Hicks emphasized that the doctrine only applies to plainly obvious evidence, and officers cannot manipulate objects to determine if they are evidence of a crime without a warrant.

In the Hicks case, officers entered an apartment without a warrant to investigate a shooting. They observed expensive stereo equipment that they suspected was stolen. To verify this suspicion, an officer moved the equipment to check serial numbers, which led to the discovery that the items were indeed stolen. The Court held that this search was unconstitutional because the officer's action of moving the equipment exceeded the bounds of the plain view doctrine. The incriminating nature of the evidence was not immediately apparent until the officer conducted further inspection, which required a warrant.

Practical Example: An officer pulls a vehicle over for a traffic violation. As the officer approaches the car, they see a bag of illegal drugs on the passenger seat in plain view. Since the officer has a legal reason to be at the vehicle (the traffic stop), and the drugs are immediately recognizable as contraband, the officer can seize the drugs without a warrant under the plain view doctrine.

6. Special Needs Exceptions

The special needs doctrine is applied in situations where searches or seizures are conducted not for the primary purpose of criminal investigation but to serve some broader governmental or societal need. This doctrine is intended to address situations where obtaining a warrant or establishing probable cause would be impractical, yet a compelling need justifies the intrusion into privacy. Special needs searches are often conducted to promote public safety, maintain order, or ensure compliance with regulatory schemes.

For example, in the 1990 case of Michigan Department of State Police v. Sitz, the Supreme Court held that sobriety checkpoints are constitutional under the Fourth Amendment. The Court held that the state's interest in reducing drunk driving and protecting public safety justified the minimal intrusion on motorists. The primary purpose was not to investigate crimes but to ensure roadway safety, thus qualifying under the special needs doctrine. In the 2002 case of Board of Education v. Earls, the Court upheld the constitutionality of drug testing for all middle and high school students participating in extracurricular activities. The Court found that the school district's interest in preventing drug use among students justified the testing policy. Given the reduced expectation of privacy for students in school settings and the importance of preventing drug use, the policy was deemed reasonable under the special needs doctrine.

There are a variety of situations where a warrantless search or seizure can be valid under the special needs exception, however, it is rare that these types of searches manifest in everyday police interactions. Nonetheless, it is important to be aware of this exception should you ever encounter it through your own police interaction.

Practical Example: At an airport, all passengers are required to go through a security checkpoint, which involves passing bags through an X-ray machine and walking through a metal detector. The primary purpose of these searches is not to detect crimes for prosecution but to ensure public safety and prevent terrorist attacks. Given the compelling governmental interest and the reduced expectation of privacy when entering an airport, these searches are justified under the special needs doctrine.

Searches and seizures are often the most contentious aspect of police interactions, but understanding the legal nuance of these concepts and how they practically apply to everyday police encounters is a necessary element of successfully navigating these encounters. While search and seizure are major aspects of the Fourth Amendment, there is another element of this amendment that must be acknowledged in the context of police interactions: the distinction between public and private property.

Public Property and Private Property

Understanding the distinction between private and public property is essential when navigating interactions with law enforcement officers. This distinction not only affects your rights but also influences the authority and limitations of police officers during encounters. As we have discussed in this chapter, the Constitution provides robust protections against unreasonable searches and seizures, particularly within the sanctity of one's private property. However, these protections vary significantly depending on whether you are on private or public property. Grasping these nuances can empower you to assert your rights appropriately and ensure that you engage with law enforcement in a manner that protects your interests.

Private property, particularly your home, is afforded the highest level of protection under the Fourth Amendment. The Supreme Court has consistently held that the home is a sacred place where privacy expectations are essentially guaranteed. In the landmark 1980 case of Payton v. New York, the Court ruled that the Fourth Amendment prohibits the police from making a warrantless and non-consensual entry into a suspect's home to make a routine felony arrest.

This decision underscores the fundamental principle that, without exigent circumstances or some other exception, law enforcement officers must obtain a warrant before entering a private residence. These protections extend not only to the physical structure of the home but also to its "curtilage," which is the area immediately surrounding and associated with the home.

The curtilage is considered part of the home for Fourth Amendment purposes. In the 1987 case of United States v. Dunn, the Supreme Court outlined factors to determine what constitutes curtilage, including the proximity of the area to the home, whether the area is enclosed, the nature of its uses, and the steps taken by the resident to protect the area from observation. This means that areas like your backyard, enclosed porch, or driveway may be protected, limiting law enforcement's ability to intrude without a warrant. However, it's important to recognize that not all areas of private property receive the same level of protection.

Open fields, for instance, do not carry an expectation of privacy, even if they are privately owned. In the 1984 case of Oliver v. United States, the Supreme Court held that open fields are not protected by the Fourth Amendment, allowing law enforcement officers to enter and search these areas without a warrant or probable cause. The rationale is that open fields are accessible to anyone and lack the intimate activities associated with the home and its curtilage.

It should also be noted that, although your home is highly protected by the Fourth Amendment, it does not serve as a safe haven from crimes, whether they're committed on your property or in public. For example, if an officer tries to stop you for committing a traffic infraction, you cannot pull into your driveway as a means of escaping the officer. The officer would be well within their authority to conduct a traffic stop in your driveway. Likewise, if officers witness a crime taking place on your property, they are not barred from entering your property to address the crime.

On the other hand, public property and public spaces present a different set of legal considerations. Public property includes spaces like streets, parks, government buildings, and other areas that are generally open and accessible to the public. In these spaces, the expectation of privacy is significantly diminished. Law enforcement officers have broader authority to observe, approach, and interact with individuals without the constraints that apply within private property. For example, activities conducted in plain view in a public space can be observed by the police without constituting a search under the Fourth Amendment. However, even in public spaces, individuals retain certain constitutional protections.

The Fourth Amendment still requires that any search or seizure be reasonable. This means that while police may engage with individuals, detain them briefly for questioning, or conduct a pat-down for weapons if they have reasonable suspicion, they cannot conduct arbitrary searches or detentions without justification. The standard for reasonable suspicion or probable cause doesn't necessarily change, but Fourth Amendment protections are generally lower in public spaces. Which means that officers have more opportunity to observe you legally without it qualifying as a Fourth Amendment search. Being in public can lead to a greater likelihood of an officer establishing probable cause or reasonable suspicion.

It's also important to be aware of the doctrine of implied consent in this context. Businesses that are open to the public, such as retail stores or restaurants, implicitly allow members of the public, including law enforcement, to enter during business hours. In these spaces, the police can enter without a warrant as any other customer would. However, their ability to search nonpublic areas or private offices within the establishment without consent or a warrant is limited by the same constitutional protections that apply to private property.

Understanding your rights during police interactions on private property also involves recognizing the limitations of police authority in certain situations. For instance, if you are renting a property, your landlord does not have the authority to consent to a search of your premises on your behalf. The Supreme Court affirmed in the 1961 case of Chapman v. United States that a landlord cannot consent to the search of a tenant's home. Similarly, hotel owners cannot consent to the search of a guest's room during the period of occupancy. However, areas considered common or shared spaces, such as apartment building hallways or lobbies, may not carry the same expectation of privacy.

Courts have often ruled that these areas are accessible to others, including law enforcement, and therefore do not provide the same Fourth Amendment protections as the interior of a private residence. This means that police may enter these common areas without a warrant and make observations that could contribute to probable cause. It is important to note that if multiple individuals share control over a property, such as roommates or family members, any one of them may consent to a search of common areas. However, they cannot consent to the search of private spaces exclusively controlled by another individual. The Supreme Court's decision in the 2006 case of Georgia v. Randolph held that if one occupant consents to a search but another present occupant expressly refuses consent, the search is invalid as to the objecting occupant.

Obtaining a nuanced understanding of how private and public property distinctions affect your rights and the authority of law enforcement can seem tedious, but it can serve as a valuable tool in the informed citizen's toolbelt to combat against police misconduct. On private property, especially within your home and its curtilage, you enjoy the highest expectation of privacy, and the police generally need a warrant to conduct searches or seizures.

On public property, your expectation of privacy is diminished, and law enforcement has broader authority to engage with you based on reasonable suspicion or probable cause. Understanding this distinction can heavily influence how you choose to respond to any given police interaction, and I highly recommend diving deeper into the cases mentioned in this section.

The Fourth Amendment protects you from unreasonable searches and seizures, but what exactly counts as "reasonable" can get complicated. It often comes down to specific legal standards that guide police actions. This is where reasonable suspicion and probable cause come into play. These concepts determine when law enforcement officers can legally stop, search, or detain you, and they are at the heart of how your rights are put into practice. In the next chapter, we'll break down what reasonable suspicion and probable cause mean, how they are applied, and what you need to know to protect yourself during police encounters.

Chapter Three
Reasonable Suspicion and Probable Cause

O n the brisk holiday afternoon of October 31, 1963, Cleveland police detective Martin McFadden was patrolling the downtown area in plain clothes when he noticed two men who failed to make eye contact with him standing on a nearby street corner. The men would later be identified as John Terry and Richard Chilton. Detective McFadden later testified that he had never seen the men before, and he was unable to say precisely what drew his attention to them.

McFadden had been a policeman for 39 years and a detective for 35 years, and had patrolled the downtown area of Cleveland for 30 of those years. McFadden would later explain that he had developed a habit of observing people in the time he spent on patrol, and told the court that he would "stand and watch people or walk and watch people at many intervals of the day." The only elaboration to his suspicions that the detective could add is that the two men "didn't look right to me at the time."

McFadden walked a bit further to gain a vantage point, and posted himself at the entrance of a store approximately 350 feet from the two men. He saw one of the men leave the other and walk southwest on Huron Road where he paused for a moment to peer into a store window. The man passed the store and walked a short distance before turning around to walk back to the corner and pausing to look into the store once again.

The man then walked back to the corner to speak to his associate and the two men began taking turns walking down the street and peeking into the store window. The men made about a dozen trips to look into the store, and at one point McFadden witnessed a third man, Carl Katz, approach the two and engage in a brief conversation before walking off in a different direction. The other two men followed shortly after.

By this time Detective McFadden had become thoroughly suspicious, and he would later testify that he suspected the men of casing the store for a robbery. Terry and Chilton began walking away, and met up with Katz down the street. McFadden decided to follow them, and later told the court that he felt that it was his duty to investigate their activities and that he feared "they may have a gun." Once the three men were reunited McFadden decided it was time to act. McFadden approached the men, identified himself as a police officer, and asked them for their names.

When one of the men "mumbled something" in response, McFadden grabbed Terry, spun him around and patted down the outside of his clothing. In Mr. Terry's left breast pocket McFadden felt a pistol. He reached inside to grab the weapon, but was unable to pull it from the coat that Mr. Terry was wearing. McFadden then ordered the three men into a nearby store where he retrieved the firearm, and conducted pat-down searches on the remaining two. He seized another pistol from the pocket of Chilton, but Katz was unarmed.

Detective McFadden testified that he only patted the men down to see if they were armed, and that he did not go into their pockets until he felt the weapons. McFadden also claimed that he never searched beyond Katz's outer garments because he did not feel a weapon during the exterior pat down. All three of the men were taken to the police station, and Terry and Chilton were charged with carrying a concealed weapon.

Terry and Chilton both filed motions to suppress the firearms as evidence at trial, but the prosecution claimed that the weapons had been seized via a search incident to a lawful arrest. The court rejected the notion that Detective McFadden had probable cause to arrest the men before he conducted the pat down search, but denied their motion anyway on the the grounds that McFadden was an experienced police officer and "had reasonable cause to believe that the defendants were conducting themselves suspiciously, and some interrogation should be made of their action."

The court held that Detective McFadden had a legitimate cause to pat down the men for his own protection because he reasonably believed the men may be armed. The court of the infamous Terry v. Ohio case went on to create a distinction between, and parameters for, investigatory stops and arrests, and laid the foundation for what would later be known as a Terry Frisk.

After being denied the motion to suppress the weapons as evidence, Terry and Chilton waived their right to a trial by jury and pleaded not guilty to the charges. The court found them guilty and the Court of Appeals for the Eighth Judicial District Affirmed the decision. Terry and Chilton appealed the decision to the Supreme Court of Ohio, who denied the appeal on the basis that no "substantial constitutional question" was proposed. The Supreme Court of the U.S. then granted certiorari "to determine whether the admission of the revolvers in evidence violated petitioner's rights under the Fourth Amendment."

The Supreme Court acknowledged that the question of whether police have the authority to stop and frisk suspicious persons is one that "thrusts to the fore difficult and troublesome issues regarding a sensitive area of police activity," and is "reflective of the tensions involved are the practical and constitutional arguments pressed with great vigor on both sides of the public debate." Prior to the Terry case, the court had never set a precedent regarding the exact limits of police authority when dealing with suspicious activity, and the basis for a stop was built upon the notion that an officer or a reliable complainant had significant evidence to prove that a crime is, has, or is going to occur. The justices understood that the precedent that was to be set in the Terry case would be one that would dramatically impact the way in which police officers carried out their duties.

The court recognized that "it is frequently argued that in dealing with the rapidly unfolding and often dangerous situations on city streets the police are in need of an escalating set of flexible responses, graduated in relation to the amount of information they possess," and also considered the opposing argument that "the authority of the police must be strictly circumscribed by the law of arrest and search as it has developed to date in the traditional jurisprudence of the Fourth Amendment." The Supreme Court realized that the Terry case had the potential to establish where the boundaries of the Fourth Amendment rest between police duty and civil liberties, and settle long standing debates regarding the applicability of the search and seizure clause at the heart of the Fourth Amendment's protections.

Noting that "Through a series of acts, each of them perhaps innocent in itself, but which taken together warranted further investigation," the court explained that while none of the men's actions were illegal they were, nonetheless, suspicious. The court went on to say that "in justifying the particular intrusion the police officer must be able to point to specific and articulable facts which, taken together with rational inferences from those facts, reasonably warrant that intrusion," and concluded that if Detective McFadden, with his 30 years of experience, had failed to investigate the men's actions then it would have been "poor police work."

The court then hinged on the notion that police work is inherently dangerous and said that "When an officer is justified in believing that the individual whose suspicious behavior he is investigating at close range is armed and presently dangerous to the officer or to others, it would appear to be clearly unreasonable to deny the officer the power to take necessary measures to determine whether the person is in fact carrying a weapon and to neutralize the threat of physical harm." In quoting the 1967 case of Warden v. Hayden the court clarified that "A search for weapons in the absence of probable cause to arrest, however, must, like any other search, be strictly circumscribed by the exigencies which justify its initiation."

The court essentially concluded that when an officer reasonably suspects an individual may be a threat to their safety then they may conduct an exterior pat down for weapons, and that a brief investigatory stop by an officer is valid so long as the officer can point to specific facts which led him to believe that criminal activity was afoot. The court went into great detail to explain that Terry stops must be brief and minimally intrusive, and that pat down searches should only apply incident to an officer's suspicion that the subject is armed and dangerous.

Over the next 25 years many courts deciphered the Terry case and applied its logic universally in cases involving Fourth Amendment violations by police. Each interpretation applied the Terry doctrine with dubious and controversial conclusions, and slowly chipped away at the balance of civil liberty and governmental intrusion that the Supreme Court had hoped to clearly establish.

In what many consider to be a sister case to the Terry ruling, the 1968 Supreme Court case of Sibron v. New York further clarified the boundaries for reasonable suspicion. In the case, an officer witnessed the defendant conversing with several known drug addicts over the course of eight hours. After watching the defendant enter a restaurant and speak to three more drug addicts the officer confronted the defendant and said "You know what I am after." When the defendant mumbled something and reached into his pocket, the officer lunged for the pocket and pulled out a bag of heroin.

The court held that the officer's observations did not meet the reasonable suspicion standard set forth in the Terry case, and concluded that "the inference that persons who talk to narcotics addicts are engaged in the criminal traffic in narcotics is simply not the sort of reasonable inference required to support an intrusion by the police upon an individual's personal security." The court reasoned that for all the officer knew, the supposed drug addicts "might have been talking about the World Series," rather than engaged in narcotics trafficking. An officer's instincts alone would not suffice to serve as justification for a Terry stop, and the Sibron case served as a prototype for distinguishing between a mere hunch and a legitimate suspicion backed by articulable facts.

Eleven years later the Supreme Court would address the boundaries of the Terry ruling once again in the 1979 case of Brown v. Texas. The Texas officers observed Brown and another man walking away from one another in an area with a high incidence of drug traffic. One officer testified that the situation "looked suspicious, and we had never seen that subject in that area before." The officers stopped Brown and demanded that he identify himself, when he refused the officers arrested him and charged him with failing to provide identification during a lawful stop.

The Supreme Court held that the circumstances preceding the stop did not give rise to reasonable suspicion, and that being in a high crime area in and of itself is not grounds to justify an intrusion from police officers. This case began the 'compounding' element of reasonable suspicion. Although being in a high crime area is not, standing alone, inherently suspicious, it may be a factor when compounded with other factors. For example: Being in a high crime area at midnight while dressed in all black and running down the street could amount to reasonable suspicion.

After the Brown ruling, interpretations of the Terry doctrine began to take a turn in the courts, and relied less on evidence and objective observations. Two years after the Brown case, the Supreme Court began to make amendments to the Terry ruling, and reshaped the nature of its applicability.

In the 1981 case of United States v. Cortez officers stopped the defendant under the suspicion that he was smuggling illegal aliens into the United States from Mexico. The officers had not observed any illegal activity, but did witness legal activity that was consistent with the smuggling of illegal aliens. The Supreme Court used the Cortez case to further develop the notion of considering the 'totality of circumstances' when deciding whether reasonable suspicion exists. Along with the observations of the officers, the court considered police reports and "patterns of operation of certain kinds of lawbreakers." The Supreme Court instructed lower courts to defer to the judgment of police officers, and recognized that "a trained officer draws inferences and makes deductions-inferences and deductions that might well elude an untrained person."

The court held that officers must be allowed to come to common sense conclusions based on their observations, and that courts should consider the legitimacy of Terry stops "not in terms of library analysis by scholars, but as understood by those versed in the field of law enforcement." The Cortez case shifted the narrative of the Terry ruling from whether a reasonable *person* would consider certain actions suspicious to whether a reasonable *officer* would find the actions suspicious. This precedent essentially handed officers the benefit of the doubt on a silver platter, and crafted a deeply seated deference for officer experience.

The Cortez case allowed members of law enforcement to draft 'expert profiles' for individuals who may be engaged in certain illegal activities, and the Supreme Court had established that individuals stopped by police do not need to be engaged in overtly illegal activity in order for the reasonable suspicion standard to apply. So long as the individual's actions fit into certain categories of behavior that, according to law enforcement experience, was likely involved in criminal activity, police would be within their authority to detain that person. This notion was reaffirmed in the 1989 Supreme Court case of United States v. Sokolow.

In the 1990 case of Michigan Department of State Police v. Sitz, the Supreme Court further chipped away at the Terry doctrine's requirement of reasonable suspicion, and gave officers even more leeway to conduct baseless stops. In the case, officers established a roadway checkpoint with the objective of capturing drunk drivers. Each stop was made without any evidence that the driver may be under the influence of any substances, and the court justified the roadblock by weighing the interest of the state to remove drunk drivers from the road against the minimal nature of the stop's intrusion upon the liberty of the citizens passing through it.

Once again the court held officer experience in high regard and stated that "For purposes of Fourth Amendment analysis, the choice among such reasonable alternatives remains with the governmental officials who have a unique understanding of, and a responsibility for, limited public resources, including a finite number of police officers." The court essentially concluded that officers should be trusted to do their job in the most effective manner possible, and what appears to be a violation of a citizen's Fourth Amendment rights could very well be the most effective way of alleviating those very citizens of more pressing dangers, such as drunk drivers.

Three years after the Sitz ruling the Supreme Court once again took on a new aspect of the reasonable suspicion doctrine in the case of Minnesota v. Dickerson. In the case, two police officers witnessed the defendant leave an apartment building that was frequently involved in drug activity. When the defendant exited the apartment complex and noticed the officers he abruptly changed directions and began walking away from them. The officers approached the defendant and ordered him to submit to a pat down search. The search revealed no weapons, but the officer conducting it testified that he felt a small lump in the respondent's jacket pocket, and believed it to be a lump of crack cocaine upon examining it with his fingers. The officer then reached into the defendant's pocket and retrieved a small bag of cocaine.

Minnesota's courts struggled to reach a consensus on the case, and the Supreme Court granted certiorari. The most prevalent question posed to the court was whether or not contraband discovered by an officer using only his sense of touch could be admitted into evidence. The Court held that officers may seize evidence found during a Terry frisk, as long as it was found during the limited search for weapons. This includes nonthreatening contraband detected through the sense of touch during a protective patdown search, so long as the primary motive of the search was for weapons and the incriminating nature of the object is immediately apparent.

The Minnesota Court of Appeals held that the officers were within their authority to stop Dickerson based solely on the fact that he was in a high crime area and his actions were evasive, and the Minnesota Supreme Court agreed. This set a precedent for lower courts to follow that essentially amounts to "location plus evasion equals reasonable suspicion." Although this decision is seemingly innocuous, it is important to bear in mind that what constitutes a 'high crime area' is often based on an officer's experience, and it can be difficult to prove whether an area is legitimately crime ridden to the point that anything appearing out of the ordinary should be investigated.

Another point to consider is that objectively provable high crime areas often exist in locations with a concentration of individuals of lower socioeconomic status. This creates a perpetual cycle of police arresting individuals who avoid them in high crime areas, and citizens avoiding police in high crime areas so that they are not arrested.

Not all lower courts share the same sentiments regarding location plus evasion equaling reasonable suspicion, but it is certainly a common theme amongst many circuits, and officers often get away with such an excuse because the primary group associated with these kinds of stops do not have the financial resources to defend themselves in court. This line of reasoning essentially amounts to requiring an officer to observe just two articulable facts in order to satisfy the reasonable suspicion standard.

No matter where you are or what you are doing a police officer must possess enough articulable facts to meet the reasonable suspicion standard in order to lawfully stop you and conduct a pat down search for weapons, however, some states also allow their officers to demand that you identify yourself along with the detainment and search. The constitutionality of these so-called 'Stop-and-Identify' statutes was affirmed in the 2004 Supreme Court case of Hiibel v. Sixth Judicial District Court of Nevada. The events of the Hiibel case perfectly demonstrate a practical application of the reasonable suspicion standard and how the Court further interpreted its applicability to identification laws.

On the afternoon of May 21, 2000, the Humboldt County Sheriff's Department received a report of a man assaulting a woman in a red and silver GMC truck on Grass Valley Road.

Deputy Sheriff Lee Dove was dispatched to investigate, and he eventually located a truck matching the description parked on the side of the road. As he exited his patrol car he observed skid marks in the gravel behind the truck, leading him to believe that it had come to a sudden stop. A man was standing by the vehicle, and a young woman was sitting inside it. The officer approached the man and began explaining that he was investigating a report before noticing that the man was intoxicated.

The officer asked the man for his identification, but the man refused and asked why the officer wanted to see his ID. The officer responded that he was conducting an investigation and needed to see the man's identification. The man insisted that he had done nothing wrong and continued to refuse the officer's request and grow increasingly agitated. Eventually the man began taunting the officer by placing his hands behind his back and insisting that he be taken to jail, to which the officer obliged, and the man was arrested and charged under Nevada Revised Statute §199.280 for "willfully resisting, delaying, or obstructing a public officer in discharging or attempting to discharge any legal duty of his office."

Larry Dudley Hiibel was the man arrested on Green Valley Road that afternoon, and the woman inside the truck was his daughter Mimi Hiibel. Larry would go on to appeal his case all the way to the Supreme Court, arguing that the requirement that he identify himself to any police officer upon request violated the Fourth Amendment prohibition on unreasonable searches and seizures and his Fifth Amendment rights against self-incrimination, which we will discuss later. There was no doubt that the officer was within their authority to stop and investigate Mr. Hiibel as he certainly had obtained reasonable suspicion upon arriving at the scene.

When the officer arrived, he located a truck matching the description and location of the information provided by the caller, which qualifies as an articulable observation that would contribute to satisfying the reasonable suspicion standard. He also noticed the tire tracks which, when complemented by his experience as an officer, could suggest that the vehicle had been dangerously stopped. As mentioned before, as little as two factors could satisfy the reasonable suspicion standard to a court, and the officer was well within his authority to investigate the scene before he even exited his patrol car.

Once the officer determined that Mr. Hiibel was intoxicated, there was no question about whether or not he was within his authority to detain and frisk him for weapons, however, the demand to see identification was not an element of the precedent originally set by the Terry case, and this aspect of the Hiibel case is how it reached the Supreme Court.

The Court had previously struck down the application of a stop-and-identify law in the 1979 case of Brown v. Texas, ruling that the Fourth Amendment requires the reasonable suspicion standard to be met before an individual can be compelled to identify themself. In the Hiibel case, there was no question concerning legitimacy of the officer's reasonable suspicion, so the Supreme Court had an ample opportunity to discuss whether stop and identify laws were consistent with the Fourth Amendment as a whole.

Section 171.123 of the Nevada Revised Statutes, which defines the authority and duties of a police officer in the context of an investigative stop, was the law in question, and the relevant subsections read as follows:

"1. Any peace officer may detain any person whom the officer encounters under circumstances which reasonably indicate that the person has committed, is committing or is about to commit a crime...

3. The officer may detain the person pursuant to this section only to ascertain his identity and the suspicious circumstances surrounding his presence abroad. Any person so detained shall identify himself, but may not be compelled to answer any other inquiry of any peace officer."

The Nevada Supreme Court had interpreted the "shall identify himself" portion of the statute to mean that "The suspect is not required to provide private details about his background, but merely to state his name to an officer when reasonable suspicion exists," and the US Supreme Court agreed, holding that "As we understand it, the statute does not require a suspect to give the officer a driver's license or any other document. Provided that the suspect either states his name or communicates it to the officer by other means." The Court went on to note that "The principles of Terry permit a State to require a suspect to disclose his name in the course of a Terry stop," and that the officer's request for identification was "a commonsense inquiry, not an effort to obtain an arrest for failure to identify after a Terry stop yielded insufficient evidence."

Ultimately the Court determined that the stop, the request, and the State's requirement of response did not interfere with Mr. Hiibel's Fourth Amendment rights, and Nevada's stop-

and-identify statute survived constitutional scrutiny on these grounds. Over the years following the Hiibel ruling many other states adopted similar stop-and-identify statutes, and 26 states now have stop-and-identify laws on the books in some form. Many states that don't have stop-and-identify statutes can still charge citizens with obstruction of justice, or a similar crime, for refusing to identify themselves

Because the development of reasonable suspicion relies heavily on a consideration of the totality of circumstances, different courts may have differing opinions regarding what exactly constitutes reasonable suspicion. in the 2001 case of U.S. v. Chavez-Valenzuela, the Ninth Circuit Court of Appeals, which has jurisdiction over California, Nevada, Alaska, and several other western states, held that because encounters with police officers are necessarily stressful for law-abiders and criminals alike, "nervousness during a traffic stop — even the extreme nervousness Chavez-Valenzuela exhibited here — in the absence of other particularized, objective factors, does not support a reasonable suspicion of criminal activity, and does not justify an officer's continued detention of a suspect after he has satisfied the purpose of the stop."

On the other hand in the 2018 case of United States v. Santillan, the Second Circuit Court of Appeals held that a police officer conducting a traffic stop had reasonable suspicion to extend the stop merely because the defendant and the driver appeared nervous and were unable to provide information about where they were coming from. Although these cases are not necessarily in direct conflict with one another, they demonstrate the varying weight of nervousness between different courts.

It should be noted that, in the 2013 Fourth Circuit case

of United States v. Black, the Court rejected the notion that reasonable suspicion can be formed by "patching together a set of innocent, suspicion-free facts, which cannot rationally be relied on to establish reasonable suspicion," emphasizing that some criminal element must exist to develop reasonable suspicion.

The legalization of medicinal and recreational marijuana has also motivated states to alter their perspectives regarding the factors supporting reasonable suspicion. The odor of marijuana alone once served as justification for a detainment and search, however, many states that have legalized marijuana have also determined that the odor of marijuana is no longer associated with criminal activity, and thus, cannot be used to develop reasonable suspicion.

Reasonable Suspicion Recap

Reasonable suspicion is the legal standard that a police officer must meet in order to stop a citizen, conduct a pat down search for weapons, and, in some states, demand a citizen's name or identification, and was first established in the 1968 Supreme Court case of Terry v. Ohio.

In order to satisfy the reasonable suspicion standard, an officer must witness behavior or possess knowledge that leads them to believe that a crime is, has, or will be committed.

Contrary to popular belief, an officer does not need to point to a specific crime that they suspect a citizen of committing. The Supreme Court has ruled that seemingly innocent behavior can be considered suspicious under certain circumstances. However, innocent facts alone are not enough and there must be some potentially criminal element to those facts.

The legality of reasonable suspicion is determined from the officer's knowledge and perspective at the time of the encounter. The Supreme Court has acknowledged that there will be instances where innocent citizens are briefly detained due to unfortunate circumstances, such as matching the description of a suspect. Simply being at the wrong place at the wrong time can result in being legally detained for something you had nothing to do with.

Reasonable suspicion must be supported by relevant factors that an officer is capable of articulating to a court, such as an officer's observations or information provided by a 911 caller.

It is important to note that, while officers are required to satisfy the reasonable suspicion standard in order to lawfully detain you, they do not have to prove that they have met that standard before they can detain you. Police officers are under no legal obligation to tell you why you have been stopped or what evidence they possess to validate your detainment, and the only time that an officer is required to justify their actions or articulate their evidence is in court.

An officer needs as little as two factors to satisfy the reasonable suspicion standard, each of which, on their own, could considered totally innocent behavior.

While simply being in a high crime area, in and of itself, is not illegal, and purposefully avoiding members of law enforcement in public is also not illegal, the Supreme Court has ruled that being in a high crime area and evading the police is enough evidence to meet the reasonable suspicion standard when combined. This illustrates how alarmingly low the bar for satisfying reasonable suspicion can be.

Each factor presented by an officer will be analyzed considering the totality of the circumstances involved in the encounter, and whether a reasonable officer in the same situation would have behaved in a similar manner.

All interactions involving a dispute of whether an officer had reasonable suspicion or not are considered on a case-by-case basis, and the courts will examine all of the facts involved in the encounter based on the evidence available to them and the statements of the parties involved. The courts will analyze the actions of the citizens as thoroughly as it will the actions of the officers involved, and it is important to bear in mind how your behavior may translate to the courtroom. It is entirely possible to be convicted of some, if not all, of the crimes you are charged with even if the original arrest is found to be unlawful.

Once an officer has acquired reasonable suspicion, they may stop and frisk you, but they cannot arrest you or search your pockets or belongings until they have obtained a higher degree of evidence known as 'probable cause.'

Probable Cause

Probable cause is the legal standard that, with some exceptions, must be met before police can make an arrest, conduct a search, or receive a warrant. The Fourth Amendment requires that any arrest be based on probable cause and plainly states that "no warrants shall issue, but upon probable cause," however, it does not specify what probable cause actually means.

Much like reasonable suspicion, probable cause is imprecise, fluid, highly dependent on context, and must be analyzed on a case-by-case basis. The concept of probable cause is very similar to reasonable suspicion, as it must be supported by objective facts that indicate a reasonable person would believe that a crime was in the process of being committed, had been committed, or was going to be committed.

In the 1949 case of Brinegar v. United States the Supreme Court defined probable cause as "where the facts and circumstances within the officers' knowledge, and of which they have reasonably trustworthy information, are sufficient in themselves to warrant a belief by a man of reasonable caution that a crime is being committed." Although the standard for probable cause is higher than that of reasonable suspicion, when exactly reasonable suspicion evolves into probable cause is difficult to determine without a court ruling. In the 1983 Supreme Court case of Illinois v. Gates the Court held that probable cause was a "practical, nontechnical conception" that is "the factual and practical considerations of everyday life on which reasonable and prudent men, not legal technicians, act." The Court noted that probable cause does not operate on the basis of absolute certainties, but more so on the rational inferences that can be drawn from objectively observable facts.

The Gates Court went on to reason that "In dealing with probable cause...as the very name implies, we deal with probabilities." As with reasonable suspicion, quantifying the concept of probable cause is nearly impossible, and the Gates Court was certain to acknowledged as much by stating "probable cause is a fluid concept -- turning on the assessment of probabilities in particular factual contexts -- not readily, or even usefully, reduced to a neat set of legal rules."

Only a court is capable of determining whether reasonable suspicion or probable cause existed at the time of a seizure, and many cases have been successfully defended by challenging the officer's suspicions. Understanding how an officer develops reasonable suspicion or probable cause can be a valuable tool for any citizen involved in a police encounter, but this information does little for a citizen when an officer doesn't understand how these concepts work. There are countless misconceptions associated with reasonable suspicion and probable cause and the individuals who perpetuate these misconceptions are both citizens and members of law enforcement alike.

Reasonable suspicion is both the literal and proverbial beginning of many police interactions, and once dispelled or disproven in court, any charges or evidence stemming from its development are likely to be dismissed. The same goes for probable cause, however, if an officer manages to successfully acquire probable cause, there is an entirely different set of legal standards regarding what they can do next.

Chapter Four
Detainment and Arrest

The processes of detainment and arrest are fundamental aspects of law enforcement, deeply rooted in the legal framework we discussed in the previous chapter. The procedures that dictate the legality of detainments and arrests are largely prescribed by constitutional principles, more specifically the amendments we discussed in chapter one. When, where, how, and for how long an officer can detain or arrest you is highly dependent on the circumstances surrounding the encounter, and it can be extremely difficult to determine if your detainment or arrest is actually lawful as it is taking place. However, determining whether or not a detainment or an arrest is lawful is only half of the puzzle, being prepared to properly respond to an unlawful detainment or arrest is another major element of successfully navigating a police interaction.

Once an encounter has evolved from a consensual encounter to a nonconsensual encounter it becomes a "detainment." As discussed in the previous chapter, officers must obtain reasonable suspicion in order to lawfully detain an individual. There are various forms of detainments, each with its own legal requirements and protocols. However, in the context of everyday police encounters, we will focus on two main types: investigative detentions and traffic stops.

Investigative Detentions

We discussed how an officer may initiate an investigative detention in the previous chapter, but the scope and limitations of investigative detentions is a relatively complex topic on its own. Once an officer has met the reasonable suspicion standard they are within their authority to initiate an investigative detention and temporarily detain a person they suspect may be committing a crime, however, there are legal standards and court rulings that limit what officers can do in the course of conducting an investigative stop.

Certain officer conduct can transform an investigative detention into what is known as a "de facto arrest," which may constitute a violation of the detainee's Fourth Amendment protections. A de facto arrest occurs when a person's freedom of movement is significantly restrained by law enforcement to a degree comparable to a formal arrest, even without a formal arrest declaration. Therefore, if an officer's conduct during an investigative detention imposes conditions that are similar to an actual arrest, such as prolonged detention or transportation to a police station, it may be considered a de facto arrest.

It is important to note that not all de facto arrests constitute a violation of the Fourth Amendment, and a de facto arrest can be justified by probable cause. However, if an officer lacks probable cause, but subjects an individual to conditions similar to an arrest, it could be a Fourth Amendment violation via de facto arrest.

As mentioned before, officers cannot make an arrest based on reasonable suspicion alone, and they must meet the standard of probable cause in order to lawfully arrest a citizen. This means that if an officer's conduct rises to the level of a de facto arrest in a situation where they only have reasonable suspicion to detain an individual but not probable cause to arrest them, a court can find that the officer violated the Fourth Amendment's prohibition on reasonable searches and seizures.

There are several notable court cases that have attempted to clarify the line between an investigative detention and an arrest, but, like most legal doctrines pertaining to police encounters, a need for a case-by-case examination of the facts of each encounter still exists. Although the totality of circumstances is a factor that must be considered, there are a few higher court cases that serve as a legal framework for investigative detentions and de facto arrests that can almost always be referred to when determining the legality of a detention.

Terry v. Ohio

As mentioned in the previous chapter, the 1968 Supreme Court case of Terry v. Ohio established the foundation for investigative detentions, which are also commonly referred to as "Terry stops." This case established that officers may initiate an investigative detention once they have met the standard of reasonable suspicion and conduct a pat-down search for weapons if they believe the person may be armed or dangerous. In many states this also authorizes officers to demand the citizen to identify themselves.

Key Point: Officers must have reasonable suspicion to detain you and pat you down for weapons. Depending on the state, they may be authorized to identify you as well.

Dunaway v. New York

In the 1979 case of Dunaway v. New York the Supreme Court held that taking a citizen to a police station for questioning without probable cause constituted an arrest, not an investigative detention, and therefore violated the Fourth Amendment. The Court emphasized that the scope of an investigative detention must not intrude upon a person's liberty beyond what is necessary to effectuate the stop. This case clarified that investigative detentions are meant to be brief and serve a specific purpose, and that removing a detainee from their original location to further their detention amounts to a de facto arrest.

Key Point: If the police detain you for an investigative detention they cannot keep you for longer than is necessary for the investigation or remove you from your original location.

Place, Sharpe, and Montoya de Hernandez

Like many other aspects of detention, the amount of time an officer can detain you is largely based on the totality of the circumstances surrounding the detention. In the 1983 Supreme Court case of United States v. Place, the Court determined that a detention of a citizen's luggage that lasted 90 minutes was too long to constitute an investigative detention and had evolved into a de facto arrest. However, the Court also clarified that there is no rigid time limit for a Terry stop and that the key consideration is whether the police diligently pursued a means of investigation likely to confirm or dispel their suspicions.

In the 1985 case of United States v. Sharpe, the Supreme Court held that a 20-minute detention was deemed reasonable given the circumstances and the officers' prompt efforts to investigate. While this case did not set a particularized standard for how long an investigative detention can be, it did clarify that 20 minutes could be considered a reasonable amount of time in certain circumstances.

The same year as the Sharpe case, the Supreme Court held that a detention of over 12 hours based on reasonable suspicion was constitutional under the circumstances in the case of United States v. Montoya de Hernandez. In the case, officers detained an individual who was suspected of attempting to traffic drugs on a flight by swallowing balloons filled with contraband. The suspect was given the option of returning to their original country on the next flight, agreeing to an x-ray, or remaining in detention until they produced a monitored bowel movement. They were unable to be placed on a flight and were eventually subjected to an anal cavity search that revealed 88 cocaine-filled balloons.

The Supreme Court found the detention reasonable, and noted that there may be special situations where a detention based on reasonable suspicion lasts a particularly long time. These rulings emphasize that the circumstances of a detention largely dictate the lawfulness of its duration.

Key Point: The amount of time an detention can last depends on the circumstances surrounding the investigation. Police stops can be as short as 20 minutes or as long as several hours depending on the nature of the case.

Minnesota v. Dickerson

The 1993 case of Minnesota v. Dickerson established that, during an investigative detention, officers are not permitted to search the pockets of the detainee unless a pat-down search reveals what could be a weapon. In the Dickerson case, the Supreme Court ruled that if an officer conducting a lawful pat-down frisk for weapons feels an object whose contour or mass makes its identity immediately apparent as contraband, the officer may lawfully seize it. However, the frisk must stay within the limits of what is necessary to detect weapons.

Officers cannot manipulate, squeeze, or otherwise further examine objects they feel during a pat-down just to determine if they're contraband. If the search exceeds these bounds, it becomes a violation of the Fourth Amendment. For example, if an officer is conducting a pat-down frisk on a suspect and they feel what is immediately apparent to be a meth pipe they would be within their authority to seize the item in question, at least temporarily. The standard for seizing an item that an officer reasonably believes to be a weapon is much lower, and does not require the item to be 'immediately apparent' as a weapon.

Key Point: When officers pat you down they cannot enter your pockets, however, if they feel something in your pocket that resembles a weapon or is immediately apparent to be contraband, they may enter the pocket to identify the item in question.

These cases collectively contribute to defining the boundaries of permissible police conduct during investigative detentions, and ensuring that such detentions remain reasonable and within the scope intended by the Fourth Amendment. Understanding the limitations of investigative detentions is a necessary element of successfully navigating a police encounter, but an entirely different set of legal standards apply for detentions that happen on the roadway.

Traffic Stops

A traffic stop, by its very nature, is a detainment and must be supported by at least reasonable suspicion. Many of the same rules and legal standards that apply to investigative detentions also apply to traffic stops, but there are some key differences. A traffic stop is an entirely different scenario to being approached by an officer on the street, and the courts have developed specific doctrines to address the unique aspects of these encounters.

During a traffic stop, officers have the authority to check the driver's license, registration, and proof of insurance as part of their investigation into the observed traffic violation, but there are also other variables at play such as passenger's rights, vehicle searches, and the use of canine units that make the legalities of traffic stops relatively nuanced. A few notable higher court cases shape the legalities surrounding traffic stops, and understanding these cases will provide practical knowledge for navigating what is, by far, the most common type of police interaction.

Delaware v. Prouse

In the 1979 case of Delaware v. Prouse, a police officer stopped a citizen's vehicle without observing any traffic violation or having any specific reasonable suspicion of criminal activity. The officer claimed that the purpose of the stop was to check the driver's license and registration, and that no traffic infractions had occurred. The Supreme Court ruled that stopping an automobile and detaining the driver to check the driver's license and vehicle registration, without any reasonable suspicion of criminal activity or traffic violation, is unconstitutional. This means that officers cannot pull over citizens simply to check their driver's license or registration, and officers must witness (or be informed of) suspicious or criminal activity before they can initiate a traffic stop. As noted in the case by Justice Byron White:

"An individual operating or traveling in an automobile does not lose all reasonable expectation of privacy simply because the automobile and its use are subject to government regulation."

Key Point: Police officers cannot stop your car just to check your driver's license or insurance. Officers must have reasonable suspicion of a traffic infraction or some other crime in order to stop your vehicle.

Pennsylvania v. Mimms and Maryland v. Wilson

The issue of whether or not an officer can order a citizen out of their vehicle during a traffic stop is one of the most contentious and widely misunderstood aspects of traffic stops. The 1977 case of Pennsylvania v. Mimms and the 1997 case of Maryland v. Wilson have established the leading legal precedent pertaining to an officer's ability to extract occupants of a stopped vehicle.

The primary issue addressed in the case of Pennsylvania v. Mimms was whether a police officer's order for a citizen to exit his vehicle during a routine traffic stop violated the Fourth Amendment's protection against unreasonable searches and seizures. In the case, a man named Harry Mimms was pulled over by Philadelphia police officers for driving with an expired license plate. During the traffic stop, one of the officers asked Mimms to step out of the vehicle. When he complied, the officer noticed a bulge under Mimms's jacket, which led to a frisk. The frisk revealed a loaded handgun, and Mimms was subsequently charged with carrying a concealed deadly weapon and unlawfully carrying a firearm without a license.

The case eventually made it to the Supreme Court, which held that an officer's request for a driver to exit the vehicle during a lawful traffic stop is a minimal and reasonable intrusion that enhances officer safety and does not violate the Fourth Amendment. Officers can remove drivers from their vehicles during lawful traffic stops at any time, and this authority was extended to include passengers in the case of Maryland v. Wilson, which many consider to be a sister case to the Mimms ruling.

Together these cases grant officers full authority to dictate who is required to exit a stopped vehicle and who should remain inside it, so it is always in your best interest to comply with an officer's request to exit or remain inside of a vehicle during a traffic stop regardless of whether you are the driver or a passenger.

Key Point: Police officers can order you and/or your passengers to get out of your vehicle at any time during a lawful traffic stop.

Carroll v. United States and Knowles v. Iowa
Vehicle searches are another major component of traffic stops, and, as we discussed in chapter two, Carroll v. United States is one of the most influential cases regarding the search of automobiles. The central issue in the case was whether the warrantless search of an automobile based on probable cause violated the Fourth

Amendment's protection against unreasonable searches and seizures. The Court recognized that automobiles are inherently mobile, which creates practical difficulties in obtaining a warrant before conducting a search. The potential for a vehicle to quickly move out of the jurisdiction or destroy evidence necessitates a more flexible approach.

The ruling established the automobile exception to the Fourth Amendment's warrant requirement. This exception allows law enforcement officers to conduct warrantless searches of vehicles if they have probable cause to believe the vehicle contains evidence of a crime or contraband, which later became known as the "Carroll doctrine." According to the Carroll doctrine, if an officer has probable cause to believe something illegal might be inside a detained vehicle, then they are within their authority to search it, however, that does not grant officers the arbitrary authority to search vehicles at will.

The case of Knowles v. Iowa addressed whether officers had the authority to search a vehicle based solely on probable cause of a traffic violation. Although officers have some authority to search a vehicle if they arrest the driver first, officers cannot conduct a full search of a vehicle based solely on the issuance of a citation without additional probable cause or reasonable suspicion. This means that police officers cannot search your vehicle without your consent unless they suspect you of committing a crime other than the traffic infraction they initially stopped you for or they have reason to believe a weapon or evidence of a crime may be in the vehicle.

Key Point: Officers cannot search your car based on a traffic infraction unless you give them consent. In order to search your car during a traffic stop the police need probable cause of a crime other than the traffic infraction they stopped you for.

Illinois v. Caballes and Rodriguez v. United States

The use of canine police units has a long history in the United States that stretches back to the early 20th century , but the deployment of canine units expanded significantly in the 1970s, particularly with the advent of the "War on Drugs." The integration of canine units into police work has been supported by various legal rulings that hinge on the notion that police dogs are reliable and effective tools for law enforcement.

While there still exists much debate about the efficacy of canine units, the courts have ruled in favor of their use, with some limitations. The case of Illinois v. Caballes addressed whether the use of a drug-sniffing dog during a lawful traffic stop violated the Fourth Amendment, particularly when the dog sniff did not prolong the stop beyond the time necessary to issue a traffic citation. The Supreme Court ruled that the use of a drug-sniffing dog on the exterior of a vehicle during a lawful traffic stop did not violate the Fourth Amendment, and that a dog sniff conducted during a lawful traffic stop that does not extend the duration of the stop is permissible. The Court emphasized that an exterior dog sniff by a trained narcotics detection dog is not a search under the Fourth Amendment because it does not require entry into the vehicle and does not expose non-contraband items to public view.

In the eyes of the Court, citizens have a diminished expectation of privacy to the exterior of their vehicle, especially when they are involved in an investigation, so the protections provided by the Fourth Amendment are not implicated in this type of search. However, there are certain circumstances where the use of a canine unit can be a violation of the Fourth Amendment. In the case of Rodriguez v. United States the Supreme Court placed limitations on when a canine unit can be used and whether or not officers can prolong a traffic stop to conduct a drug sniff. The Court held that police may not prolong a traffic stop beyond the time reasonably required to handle the matter for which the stop was made unless they have additional reasonable suspicion of criminal activity.

The Court emphasized that the purpose of a traffic stop is to address the traffic violation that prompted the stop, such as checking the driver's license, verifying registration and insurance, and issuing a citation or warning. Any additional time spent on tasks unrelated to the traffic violation must be justified by separate reasonable suspicion. This means that an officer cannot make you wait on the side of the road while a canine unit arrives after they have completed the initial traffic stop, however, the Rodriguez case has been widely misinterpreted to mean that an officer cannot call a canine unit to a traffic stop at all, which is not the case.

As long as the officer who summons the canine unit does so as he is performing the necessary tasks to complete the traffic stop, and it arrives before the officer has completed the stop, then the officer would be within their authority to conduct an exterior sniff of the vehicle. There are always a plethora of unique variables at play during any police interaction that could impact the legality of canine searches, but it is important to be aware that the courts have typically granted officers significant leeway regarding the use of canine units and sniff searches.

Key Point: Officers can use dogs to sniff the exterior of your vehicle during a traffic stop as long as they don't extend the stop in order to do so. However, arguing that a stop was prolonged to get a dog on the scene can be difficult in court because it is up to the officer to determine when traffic stop tasks are completed and how long they take.

Brendlin v. California and Arizona v. Johnson

Another unique aspect of traffic stops is that they often involve more than one person, and the courts have directly addressed the rights of passengers during traffic stops in various rulings. Both Brendlin v. California and Arizona v. Johnson collectively enhance the legal understanding of the Fourth Amendment's application to passengers during traffic stops, and apply directly to everyday police interactions.. The Brendlin case established that a passenger in a vehicle is considered "detained" during a traffic stop, which means that they are entitled to the same Fourth Amendment protections as the driver, but also subject to the authority of the officers conducting the stop. The Johnson case granted officers further authority, allowing them to conduct a frisk of a passenger during a traffic stop if they have reasonable suspicion that the passenger is armed and dangerous, even if the officer does not have suspicion that the passenger is involved in criminal activity beyond the traffic violation.

The courts have granted officers relatively broad authority to dictate the movement and conduct of passengers during traffic stops, and it is almost always a good idea to obey the commands of an officer if you are a passenger during a traffic stop and challenge them later in court if you believe they may have been unlawful.

Key Point: Passengers are considered detained during a traffic stop and have the same rights as drivers. However, they are also subject to the authority of the officers conducting the stop.

Detentions during traffic stops are a critical aspect of law enforcement that balance the need for effective policing with the protection of individual constitutional rights. The Supreme Court rulings we discussed have clarified the boundaries within which police officers must operate and emphasize the importance of reasonable suspicion and the permissible scope of searches and frisks. Identifying an illegal detention can be a crucial element of defending against police misconduct and ensuring that evidence obtained through such stops is not unlawfully admitted in court.

Before we dive into the legal intricacies of formal arrests, it is important to note that being placed in handcuffs does not mean that you are being arrested, and officers are within their authority to handcuff citizens during an investigative detention or traffic stop to ensure officer safety during a high-risk situation. In the 1985 Supreme Court case of United States v. Hensley, the Court found that reasonable suspicion authorized officers to "take such steps as were reasonably necessary to protect their personal safety and to maintain the status quo during the course of the stop." In other words, if an officer has reasonable suspicion to believe someone might be involved in criminal activity, they are permitted to take reasonable actions—such as asking a person to remove their hands from their pockets—to make sure everyone stays safe and that the situation doesn't escalate during the stop.

In the 2005 case of Muehler v. Mena the Supreme Court held that the use of handcuffs did not violate the Fourth Amendment because it was reasonable under the circumstances to maintain officer safety during the execution of the search warrant. This case indicated that officers may employ the use of handcuffs to temporarily detain citizens during the course of an investigative detention if an officer safety issue arises, and several lower court rulings have affirmed that officers also have the authority to place citizens in the back of their patrol vehicle during the detention.

Although the courts have granted officers the authority to engage in conduct that is nearly identical to a formal arrest during an investigative detention, there is a fine line between detention and arrest that officers must tread carefully. Arrests require a higher evidentiary threshold of probable cause and trigger a different set of constitutional safeguards, shifting the way law enforcement interacts with suspects and the legal recourse available to citizens.

Arrests

Unlike detainments, arrests involve a higher level of restraint and typically lead to an individual being transported to a police station, booked, and formally charged with a crime. The primary difference between an arrest and a detainment is the level of evidence required, the extent of the restraint on the individual's freedom, and the subsequent legal processes involved.

As mentioned before, officers must meet the standard of probable cause before they can make an arrest without a warrant, which is a relatively more difficult standard to achieve than reasonable suspicion. Once they have acquired probable cause they are authorized to make an arrest by any reasonable means necessary and have much greater discretionary power to effectuate the arrest, meaning that they are authorized to use force if necessary.

Once an arrest has been made and charges are filed against an individual, it will be followed by criminal court proceedings to determine whether or not a crime was committed. The implications and repercussions of an arrest are significantly higher than those of a detention, and it is almost always in a citizen's best interest to avoid being arrested if at all possible.

Once an officer has made an arrest, the constitutional protections of the arrested citizen become somewhat diminished. People who are arrested are no longer entitled to the freedom of movement or the freedom of privacy, but this does not mean that an arrested citizen's constitutional rights are completely gone. While an arrest does restrict certain rights, it also activates others, as demonstrated by several notable cases that highlight the limitations and authority of officers during an arrest.

Beck v. Ohio and United States v. Watson

Whether or not an officer has probable cause is a crucial aspect of making a lawful arrest, and this is the element of arrests that is most often contested in the courtroom. The Supreme Court cases of Beck v. Ohio and United States v. Watson are related in their exploration and clarification of the Fourth Amendment's probable cause requirement for warrantless arrests. Both cases examine the circumstances under which law enforcement officers can constitutionally arrest a suspect without a warrant.

In the Beck case, police officers in Cleveland, Ohio, received unspecified "information" about a man named William Beck. They stopped him in his car and arrested him without a warrant for operating a "scheme of chance." During the arrest, they searched his car but found nothing of note. At the police station, however, they searched Beck further and found an envelope containing clearing house slips hidden under his sock—possession of which was illegal in Ohio. Beck was subsequently charged in Cleveland Municipal Court, but filed a motion to suppress the slips.

Beck argued that the slips were seized in violation of the Fourth and Fourteenth Amendments, but Ohio courts denied the motion after a hearing. He was convicted at trial, with the slips as the primary evidence. On appeal, both the Ohio Court of Appeals and the Ohio Supreme Court upheld his conviction, ruling that the searches were part of a lawful arrest despite the lack of a warrant. Beck appealed again and the Supreme Court overturned the decisions of the lower courts. The Court emphasized that probable cause for an arrest exists when the facts and circumstances within the officers' knowledge, and of which they have reasonably trustworthy information, are sufficient to warrant a prudent person in believing that the suspect has committed or is committing an offense. The ruling underscored that officers must be able to point to specific and articulable facts that justify their belief that an individual is involved in criminal activity, and a warrantless arrest cannot be based on unreliable or uncorroborated evidence.

The Watson case, on the other hand, noted that the practice of warrantless arrests in public places was deeply rooted in common law and had been historically accepted in both England and the United States. In this case, a man named Michael Watson was suspected of credit card fraud, based on information provided by a confidential informant. Acting on this information, a postal inspector arranged to meet Watson at a public restaurant. During the meeting, Watson was arrested without a warrant by the postal inspector. Following the arrest, Watson consented to a search of his car, during which officers found stolen credit cards.

As a result, Watson was charged with possession of stolen mail.

At trial, Watson challenged the legality of the warrantless arrest, arguing it violated his Fourth Amendment rights. The trial court rejected his argument, admitted the evidence obtained from the consensual search of his car, and convicted him. Watson then appealed to the Court of Appeals for the Ninth Circuit, which ruled in his favor, finding the warrantless arrest unconstitutional. In response, the government petitioned the Supreme Court to review the case. The Supreme Court agreed to hear it to decide whether a warrantless arrest for a felony in a public place, based on probable cause, was constitutional.

The Court concluded that the Framers of the Constitution did not intend to prohibit warrantless arrests when they adopted the Fourth Amendment, and reaffirmed that probable cause is the key requirement for such arrests. As long as officers have reasonably trustworthy information that would lead an average person to believe that a suspect has committed a felony, a warrantless arrest in a public place is permissible.

Much like reasonable suspicion, the concept of probable cause is fluid, dynamic, and highly dependent on the totality of circumstances surrounding the arrest. The Beck case and the Watson case can be seen as two ends of a spectrum of officer conduct that would support or invalidate probable cause. Both of these cases are worth reading in full if you wish to gain a deeper understanding of how the legal doctrine of probable cause is viewed through the lens of a higher court.

Key Point: Officers must have probable cause in order to make an arrest, and an arrest cannot be based on unreliable evidence.

Miranda v. Arizona

Being questioned or interrogated by the police during an arrest can have a profound impact on the legal proceedings subsequent to the arrest, and the courts have recognized that it is the government's burden to ensure that citizens understand certain rights they are entitled to during an arrest. The 1966 case of Miranda v. Arizona is fundamentally important to the practical aspects of an arrest as it established the requirement that law enforcement officers must inform individuals of their constitutional rights before conducting a custodial interrogation.

When a person is taken into custody, the police must provide a "Miranda warning," which includes informing the suspect of their right to remain silent, that anything they say can be used against them in court, their right to an attorney, and that an attorney will be provided if they cannot afford one. This guarantees that suspects are informed of their Fifth Amendment protection against self-incrimination and their Sixth Amendment right to legal counsel.

We will discuss the Miranda warning in more detail in the next chapter, but contrary to popular belief, an officer's failure to recite a Miranda warning does not render an arrest illegal or invalid. If an officer fails to provide a Miranda warning to a suspect then any information resulting from questioning or interrogation by that specific officer will not be admissible in court, but the officer's arrest is still considered lawful until proven otherwise. Typically, an individual who is arrested and interrogated by police officers or detectives is read their Miranda warning several times throughout the interrogation process, but the Miranda v. Arizona case ensures that citizens who are not informed of their rights are not subject to unlawful questioning.

It is important to note that what you say to a police officer during an investigative stop can be used against you in court, even if you have not been read your Miranda rights. A Miranda warning is required only when a person is in custody and subject to interrogation. Anything you say prior to being arrested is not protected by the Miranda ruling, and this is why it is so important to understand the right to remain silent that is guaranteed by the Fifth Amendment.

Key Point: Officers must inform you of your right to remain silent and your right to an attorney before they can interrogate you. This is not required to make an arrest and only applies to questioning that takes place after an arrest is made.

Atwater v. City of Lago Vista and Virginia v. Moore

Many misdemeanor offenses, such as minor traffic infractions, are typically handled through the issuance of a citation by an officer rather than a full scale arrest. Thousands of police interactions take place on a daily basis that result in nothing more than a citation, which is merely a promise or notice to appear before the court and answer for the alleged charges.

However, citations are a discretionary tool for police officers, not a constitutional requirement, and officers are well within their authority to make an arrest based on probable cause in most situations, regardless of the severity of the offense. Some jurisdictions have drafted statutory limitations that prohibit arrests for certain minor violations, but the Supreme Court has determined that the Constitution itself does not prohibit officers from arresting citizens for committing even the most minor offense.

In the 2001 Supreme Court case of Atwater v. City of Lago Vista, an officer stopped a citizen and ultimately arrested them for a seatbelt violation, despite the fact that the offense was punishable by a fine rather than jail time. The Supreme Court ruled that the Fourth Amendment does not prohibit a warrantless arrest for a minor criminal offense, even if the offense is punishable only by a fine. The Court concluded that as long as the officer has probable cause to believe that an individual has committed a crime, an arrest is constitutionally permissible. This decision weighed the power of probable cause heavily, and has been the subject of much legal debate.

Critics of the decision argue that it opens the door to potential misuse of arrest powers, allowing officers to arrest individuals for very minor offenses, which could lead to abuses of power and disproportionately affect marginalized communities. It should be noted that some jurisdictions have implemented policies or legislation to limit arrests for minor offenses, encouraging officers to issue citations instead, in response to the Atwater decision.

The 2008 Supreme Court case of Virginia v. Moore reinforced the principle that probable cause is the primary standard for determining whether an arrest complies with the Fourth Amendment. The Moore case determined that even if an arrest is technically illegal under state law the Fourth Amendment is not automatically violated as long as there is probable cause. The Supreme Court emphasized that the Fourth Amendment does not require police officers to follow state-specific rules regarding arrests. Instead, it imposed a federal standard of reasonableness, and under that standard, the presence of probable cause is sufficient to make a valid arrest.

The Atwater case and the Moore case collectively illustrate the broad discretionary powers granted to law enforcement officers through probable cause and their ability to conduct arrests without needing to adhere strictly to state procedural limitations.

Key Point: In some states you can be arrested for any criminal offense, even minor traffic infractions, so long as the officer has probable cause. A ticket, or citation, is an agreement that you will show up to court so that you are not arrested on the spot.

Once an officer has initiated an arrest, compliance is absolutely necessary, and there is almost no scenario where resisting an arrest will be beneficial in the long run, even if the arrest is unlawful. There are a very small minority of states where resisting an unlawful arrest is legal, however, the caveat is that the arrest must be unlawful in the eyes of a court. In the vast majority of states, resisting an arrest is illegal regardless of whether the arrest is lawful or unlawful. If a citizen mistakenly resists an arrest that is lawful then they will likely face additional charges and ruin their chances of beating the case or filing any lawsuit, which makes resisting any arrest a risky endeavor.

It is impossible to know all the facts associated with an officer's decision to effectuate a detainment or arrest, and the police are well within their authority to withhold information during an investigation. Considering the overwhelming discretionary power granted to officers during detainments and arrests, the odds of successfully resisting an arrest, lawful or not, and subsequently defending that resistance in court are extremely low, regardless of whether states have laws that support it. Unless faced with the risk of death or permanent injury, physically resisting arrest is not worth the risk of life or freedom that comes with it, and it is always better to fight your battles against police misconduct in the courtroom, not on the street.

Excessive Force

The use of excessive force has significant implications for citizens, as it can result in severe injuries, lasting psychological damage, a deep mistrust of law enforcement within communities, or even death. In the context of detainment and arrest, the issue of excessive force underscores the delicate balance between maintaining public safety and upholding constitutional rights. The courts have recognized that the use of force is a necessary element of policing, but they have also recognized that the Constitution offers citizens protections against unreasonable uses of force. Two landmark Supreme Court decisions lay the foundation upon which excessive force claims are built, and continue to play an important role in seeking justice for police misconduct.

Tennessee v. Garner

This case significantly shaped the legal standards surrounding excessive force, and continues to play a major role in excessive force claims to this day. The case addressed the constitutionality of the use of deadly force to prevent the escape of unarmed, non-dangerous suspects. In the case, Memphis police officers Leslie Wright and Elton Hymon responded to a burglary call at around 10:45 p.m. on October 3, 1974. Officer Hymon saw Edward Garner fleeing across the yard and stopping at a chain-link fence. Garner, who was 15 but appeared older to Hymon, seemed unarmed. When Garner attempted to climb the fence despite Hymon's order to halt, Hymon shot him, believing Garner would escape if he made it over.

Garner died shortly afterward, and ten dollars and a purse taken from the house were found on him. Hymon acted under Tennessee state law and Memphis Police Department policy, which allowed deadly force against fleeing suspects. Garner's father sued, arguing a violation of civil rights. The District Court upheld Hymon's actions as constitutional, but the Sixth Circuit Court of Appeals reversed, ruling that the statute failed to reasonably limit deadly force in line with the seriousness of the crime. The State of Tennessee then appealed to the Supreme Court.

The Court held that the use of deadly force to prevent the escape of a fleeing suspect is a "seizure" under the Fourth Amendment and must be reasonable, and established that deadly force is not justified unless the suspect poses a significant threat of death or serious physical injury to officers or others.

The Court introduced a balancing test to determine the reasonableness of a seizure, weighing the nature and quality of the intrusion on the individual's Fourth Amendment rights against the governmental interests at stake. For example, if an officer were to use deadly force against a fleeing shoplifter, that would be viewed differently by the courts than if an officer were to use deadly force against a fleeing mass murderer. The Garner case provides a framework for courts to evaluate the reasonableness of police use of deadly force on fleeing suspects, ensuring that such actions are subject to judicial scrutiny.

Key Point: The amount of force an officer can use on a fleeing suspect must be reasonable based on the circumstances. Officers can use a higher degree of force against fleeing suspects who pose a threat to others.

Graham v. Connor

In Graham v. Connor the Supreme Court set a standard for evaluating claims of excessive force by law enforcement under the Fourth Amendment. In the case, a man named Dethorne Graham experienced an insulin reaction and asked a friend to drive him to a convenience store to buy orange juice to counteract his condition. Graham quickly entered and exited the store, where he caught the attention of Officer Connor, who found Graham's behavior suspicious.

Officer Connor initiated a traffic stop on the vehicle and became more suspicious of Graham, as he was displaying symptoms of a diabetic shock which Officer Connor mistook to be signs of intoxication. The driver attempted to alert the officers of Graham's medical condition, but the officers ignored him and handcuffed Graham after he passed out from the insulin reaction, refusing to provide medical aid. During the encounter, Graham suffered a broken foot, cuts on his wrists, a bruised forehead, and an injured shoulder, which led him to file a lawsuit against the officers involved.

Although the Supreme Court did not directly rule on whether or not the officers in the Graham case engaged in excessive force, the case still established an important legal precedent regarding excessive force known as the "Objective Reasonableness Standard," which holds that a use of force by police must be judged from the perspective of a reasonable officer on the scene, rather than with the benefit of hindsight. The case also created what became colloquially known as the 'Graham Factors,' which is a three part test to determine whether a use of force was excessive.

The Graham Factors consider the following variables to evaluate a use of force:

1. The severity of the suspected crime: Officers may use a degree of force that is proportionate to the seriousness of the crime. For example, officers are allowed to use more force to stop a shooter versus someone who is suspected of jaywalking.

2. The immediate threat the suspect poses: If a suspect is particularly dangerous to the officers, themselves, or the public, then officers are within their authority to use a higher degree of force to prevent potential harm.

3. Active resistance or evasion: Officers may use a reasonable degree of force to prevent a suspect from resisting or evading arrest.

This decision established a concrete framework for courts to evaluate claims of excessive force, and recognized that police officers often make split-second decisions in tense, uncertain, and rapidly evolving situations. Unfortunately for Dethorne Graham, the Supreme Court sent his case back to the Fourth Circuit after establishing the Objective Reasonableness Test, where the Fourth Circuit applied the test and found that Officer Connor's use of force was reasonable.

Key Point: The amount of force an officer uses to arrest you must be reasonable based on the circumstances of the arrest.

Together, the Graham case and the Garner case offer citizens valuable insights into how the courts view the use of force by police officers, placing emphasis on the principles of objective reasonableness and the necessity of assessing the immediate threat posed by suspects. These landmark decisions establish clear legal standards that police actions must be both justified and proportionate, and mandate that force is used appropriately and only when necessary.

By understanding the guidelines set forth in these cases, citizens can better grasp their rights during police encounters and the legal boundaries within which law enforcement must operate when using force. The tenets of the Graham and Garner cases have been incorporated into nearly every police department policy in the country and continue to serve as a framework for accountability to prevent abuses of power and protect the constitutional rights of all citizens.

Understanding the legalities of detainment and arrest are absolutely essential to becoming a more informed citizen. The landmark Supreme Court cases we discussed in this chapter delineate the fine line between lawful police conduct and the infringement of individual rights during these types of encounters. By educating yourself on the principles established in these cases, you contribute to a more just and equitable society where the balance between law enforcement authority and individual rights is more fairly maintained. Awareness and understanding of your rights during detainment and arrest are essential tools for ensuring that justice and civil liberties are upheld in every encounter with law enforcement across the country.

Chapter Five
The Right to Remain Silent

I n the context of civilian rights, the Fifth Amendment holds a place of paramount importance, particularly during police encounters. It serves as a critical safeguard against self-incrimination and ensures the due process of law.

The historical roots of the Fifth Amendment trace back to English common law and the abuses of the Star Chamber, a secret court that compelled testimony through coercion and torture. The framers of the Constitution sought to prevent such governmental overreach by embedding protections that ensure fairness and respect for individual rights. The Self-Incrimination Clause, for example, embodies the principle that the government bears the burden of proof in criminal cases and cannot coerce individuals into providing evidence against themselves.

In modern times, the Fifth Amendment plays a crucial role during police interactions, particularly when officers seek to question individuals about potential involvement in criminal activity. Law enforcement officers are trained to gather information and may employ various strategies to elicit statements that could be used as evidence. It is in these moments that the protections of the Fifth Amendment become most significant, serving as a shield against involuntary self-incrimination and preserving the integrity of the legal process.

Culturally and historically, the Fifth Amendment has been both celebrated and misunderstood. Phrases like "pleading the Fifth" have entered common parlance, sometimes carrying negative connotations or assumptions of guilt. It's important to dispel these misconceptions. Asserting your Fifth Amendment rights is a lawful and prudent action that upholds the principles of justice and fairness. It is not an admission of wrongdoing but a recognition of the fundamental legal protections afforded to every individual.

At the heart of the right against self-incrimination is the presumption of innocence, which is the foundational principle that every person is considered innocent until proven guilty beyond a reasonable doubt. This presumption places the burden of proof squarely on the government, requiring prosecutors to establish guilt through evidence independently obtained, rather than through compelled testimony from the accused. By prohibiting the government from forcing individuals to testify against themselves, the Fifth Amendment upholds the integrity of the legal process and protects individual autonomy and dignity.

The principle of "innocent until proven guilty" underscores the rationale behind the right against self-incrimination. By ensuring that individuals are not compelled to contribute to their own prosecution, the legal system reinforces the notion that the government must build its case without relying on coercion. The right against self-incrimination is not merely a legal technicality but a fundamental aspect of a fair and just legal system. It serves to uphold the presumption of innocence and ensures that the burden of proof rests with the government.

As you engage with law enforcement, keeping these principles in mind can guide your actions and responses, helping you maintain control over your personal autonomy and legal rights. Knowing when and how to assert your Fifth Amendment rights can be a daunting, and potentially risky, task during a police interaction, but understanding the legal concepts and practical applications of this protection can be a valuable tool to any citizen.

Invoking the Right to Remain Silent

In the complex landscape of civilian rights, one principle stands out as both vital and often misunderstood: the necessity of explicitly invoking your right to remain silent. The Fifth Amendment guarantees that no person "shall be compelled in any criminal case to be a witness against himself," safeguarding individuals from self-incrimination. However, the practical application of this protection requires more than mere silence; it demands a clear and unambiguous assertion of your intent to exercise this right.

When confronted by police officers, many individuals believe that simply remaining silent is sufficient to invoke their Fifth Amendment rights. This assumption, while seemingly logical, does not align with the nuances of legal interpretations established by the courts.

The Supreme Court has clarified that the right to remain silent is not self-executing; in other words, you must literally declare that you are invoking your right to silence. Without an explicit declaration, your silence alone may not trigger the protections against self-incrimination, potentially leaving you vulnerable to further questioning and the use of your silence as evidence against you. Simply remaining silent during a police interaction does not invoke your right to remain silent, which means that your silence can be used as a factor for reasonable suspicion or as admissible evidence in court.

In order to invoke your right to remain silent, you must state something like "I would like to invoke my right to remain silent," or "I do not want to speak without my lawyer present." The requirement of verbally expressing your right to remain silent was underscored in the 2013 Supreme Court case of Salinas v. Texas. The Court emphasized that the privilege against self-incrimination generally must be claimed in order to be effective. This decision illustrates the critical importance of explicitly stating your intention to remain silent, rather than assuming that silence alone offers protection.

The courts have held that clear communication is necessary to prevent misunderstandings and to allow law enforcement to adjust their conduct accordingly. If officers are unaware that you are invoking your Fifth Amendment rights, they may continue questioning, potentially leading to self-incrimination or the perception that you are willingly participating in the conversation. By expressly stating your intent, you provide a clear boundary that officers are legally obligated to respect.

In the 1951 case of Hoffman v. United States, the Supreme Court determined that the privilege against testimonial compulsion "not only extends to answers that would in themselves support a conviction but likewise embraces those which would furnish a link in the chain of evidence needed to prosecute the claimant." The Court also explained that individuals do not need to answer questions when they have "reasonable cause to apprehend danger from a direct answer," and that to claim the privilege, "it need only be evident from the implications of the question, in the setting in which it is asked, that a responsive answer to the question or an explanation of why it cannot be answered might be dangerous because injurious disclosure could result." In other words, anytime a citizen reasonably feels as though their answer to a question asked by the police might be incriminating, they may invoke their right to silence.

Building on the Hoffman decision, the Supreme Court held in the 2001 case of Ohio v. Reiner that the privilege against self-incrimination applied to the innocent as well as the guilty because "truthful responses of an innocent witness, as well as those of a wrongdoer, may provide the government with incriminating evidence from the speaker's own mouth," and that, as the suspect of an investigation, it was reasonable for an individual to fear that answers to questions might incriminate them.

It's important to recognize that invoking your right to remain silent does not imply guilt. The Supreme Court has affirmed that exercising constitutional rights should not be construed as evidence of wrongdoing. In the 1965 case of Griffin v. California, the Court held that prosecutors cannot comment on a defendant's refusal to testify at trial, as it would penalize the exercise of the Fifth Amendment privilege.

Similarly, during police encounters, invoking your right is a lawful and prudent measure to protect yourself, regardless of innocence or guilt. In addition to the requirement for explicit invocation, it's crucial to understand that the right to remain silent applies in various contexts, not just during custodial interrogations after an arrest. Whether you are stopped on the street, involved in a traffic stop, or voluntarily speaking with officers, the need to assert your rights clearly remains consistent.

Police Questioning: How to Respond

Interacting with law enforcement often involves a series of questions aimed at gathering information. How you respond to these inquiries can significantly impact the outcome of the encounter and your legal standing. Understanding which questions you are obligated to answer and which you can decline is essential for safeguarding your Fifth Amendment rights against self-incrimination. Officers are trained to ask questions in a manner that encourages dialogue, sometimes blurring the line between casual conversation and investigative interrogation. Recognizing this, it's crucial to discern which questions you must answer and how to respond appropriately to those you are not obligated to address.

As discussed in previous chapters, in many jurisdictions, "stop-and-identify" statutes require individuals to provide basic identifying information during a lawful stop. This typically includes your name and, in some cases, your date of birth or address. The Supreme Court affirmed the constitutionality of these statutes in the 2004 case of Hiibel v. Sixth Judicial District Court of Nevada, where it ruled that requiring a suspect to disclose their name during a Terry stop doesn't typically violate the Fifth Amendment. The Court reasoned that stating one's name is generally not incriminating and serves a legitimate law enforcement purpose. Although the Court also acknowledged that "a case may arise where there is a substantial allegation that furnishing identity at the time of a stop would have given the police a link in the chain of evidence needed to convict the individual of a separate offense," this would be a rare defense to refusing to identify in the context of everyday police interactions.

Therefore, when an officer lawfully stops you based on reasonable suspicion of criminal activity, you are generally required to provide your name. Refusal to do so may result in legal consequences, such as arrest for obstruction or similar charges. However, beyond this basic information, you are under no obligation to answer further questions that delve into details about your activities, associations, or other potentially incriminating subjects.

When faced with questions you are not required to answer, how you respond becomes critical. The goal is to assert your rights without escalating the situation or appearing uncooperative in a manner that might provoke unnecessary tension. A respectful and calm demeanor goes a long way in maintaining a constructive interaction.

If an officer asks questions beyond basic identification, such as "Where are you coming from?" or "What are you doing here?" you can politely decline to answer. A suggested response might be, "Officer, I mean no disrespect, but I would like to remain silent so that I can avoid potentially incriminating myself." This statement clearly communicates your intention to exercise your Fifth Amendment rights without challenging the officer's authority or engaging in confrontational language.

It's important to avoid sarcasm, hostility, or accusatory tones, as these can exacerbate the situation and potentially lead to additional complications. Remember that officers are assessing not only your words but also your behavior, and maintaining composure is beneficial for both parties.

Understanding that casual conversation can lead to unintended disclosures is also essential. Officers may engage in seemingly benign dialogue to build rapport or to encourage you to lower your guard. Questions about the weather, sports, or other common topics might precede more probing inquiries.

While it may feel awkward to refrain from engaging in small talk, especially if you wish to appear cooperative, it's important to be cautious. Even innocent remarks can provide officers with information that may be used in their investigation. To navigate this, you might acknowledge the officer's comments without offering additional information. For example, if an officer mentions, "It's a nice day out, isn't it?" a simple nod or a neutral response suffices.

If the conversation shifts toward topics that could relate to criminal activity or your personal affairs, reaffirming your choice to remain silent is appropriate. Consistency in your responses helps reinforce your intent and reduces the likelihood of confusion or misinterpretation. Avoiding self-incrimination requires vigilance, particularly when officers employ open-ended questions designed to elicit detailed responses.

Questions like "Can you tell me what happened here?" or "Do you know why I stopped you?" invite you to provide explanations that may inadvertently admit fault or reveal incriminating details. It's advisable to refrain from offering explanations or justifications on the spot. Instead, you can respond by saying, "I prefer not to answer any questions without an attorney present." This approach not only asserts your Fifth Amendment rights but also signals your awareness of the legal process.

Requesting an attorney underscores your understanding that any discussion should occur within the appropriate legal context.

It's important to note that the right to counsel is protected under the Sixth Amendment and only applies after an arrest. However, expressing your desire for legal representation can still be a strategic way to emphasize your intent to protect your rights during initial interactions.

In situations where you are unsure whether you are legally required to answer a question, it's acceptable to seek clarification. You might ask, "Am I legally obligated to answer that question, officer?" This inquiry prompts the officer to specify whether the question pertains to mandatory identification or voluntary information. If the officer insists that you must answer, and you believe the request exceeds legal requirements, you can reiterate your intention to remain silent and seek legal counsel.

As we will discuss in the next chapter, it is also crucial to be aware of your body language and non-verbal cues during the encounter. Nervous gestures, fidgeting, or avoiding eye contact can sometimes be misinterpreted by officers as signs of deception or guilt. While it's natural to feel anxious, making a conscious effort to present a calm and composed demeanor can positively influence the interaction. Standing straight, maintaining a neutral facial expression, and using a clear, steady voice contribute to conveying confidence and respect.

It's also important to recognize that maintaining silence does not mean you should physically resist or obstruct the officer's actions. Compliance with lawful commands, such as providing identification or following instructions during a detention, is necessary. Physical resistance can lead to additional charges and escalate the situation unnecessarily.

Balancing assertiveness in protecting your rights with compliance in following lawful orders is key to navigating the encounter safely and effectively. Responding to police questions requires a thoughtful and informed approach that prioritizes your constitutional rights while maintaining respect and composure. By communicating your intentions clearly, avoiding self-incriminating statements, and being mindful of both verbal and non-verbal cues, you position yourself to protect your legal interests without provoking unnecessary conflict.

Use the Fifth Amendment Wisely

The Fifth Amendment empowers you with the right against self-incrimination, allowing you to decline answering questions that could be used against you in a court of law. However, invoking this right without consideration of the situational dynamics can sometimes inadvertently heighten an officer's suspicion, potentially complicating the encounter. Understanding how to exercise your right to silence judiciously, while also engaging in a manner that does not escalate tension, is essential for protecting your interests and ensuring a safe and respectful interaction.

When approached by law enforcement, your immediate response sets the tone for the entire encounter. Officers are trained to observe behavior, assess risk, and gather information efficiently. Abruptly invoking your right to silence without context or in a confrontational manner may raise red flags, leading officers to question your motives or perceive you as uncooperative. Conversely, engaging too freely in conversation can result in unintended self-incrimination or the disclosure of information that may be misconstrued. Striking the right balance requires a thoughtful approach that acknowledges the officer's role while also protecting your constitutional rights.

One effective strategy is to begin the interaction with a polite and cooperative demeanor. Simple gestures like making eye contact, keeping your hands visible, and responding to initial greetings can help establish a non-threatening atmosphere. When an officer approaches and says, "Good evening, how are you?" responding with a courteous, "I'm fine, thank you," maintains cordiality without delving into substantive discussion.

This initial engagement demonstrates respect and can ease any immediate tension, setting a foundation for a more manageable interaction. It is okay to engage in formative pleasantries with officers, as simply saying "hello" could rarely be seen as incriminating in any way, as it establishes a positive tone for the interaction. As the conversation progresses, you may be asked questions that delve into areas you prefer not to discuss.

For instance, an officer might inquire, "Where are you headed tonight?" or "Can you tell me what you're doing in this area?" These questions, while seemingly innocuous, can lead to disclosures that may not be in your best interest. To exercise your right to remain silent without exacerbating the situation, consider responding with a polite but firm statement that acknowledges the officer's role while asserting your rights. Phrases like, "Officer, I understand you're doing your job, but I prefer not to answer any questions without legal counsel," communicate your position clearly and respectfully.

It's important to avoid abrupt or dismissive remarks such as "I don't have to tell you anything" or "It's none of your business," which can be perceived as antagonistic. Such responses may escalate the encounter and potentially give rise to additional scrutiny or legal justifications for further action by the officer. Maintaining a respectful tone and choosing your words carefully can help mitigate these risks.

In situations where you feel comfortable providing limited information to dispel immediate concerns, you might opt to share benign details that do not implicate you in any wrongdoing. For example, if an officer expresses concern about recent incidents in the area, you might acknowledge awareness of the situation without offering additional information about your activities. This approach can help satisfy the officer's need for engagement while preserving your right to withhold potentially incriminating details.

In some instances, providing minimal cooperation can expedite the encounter's conclusion. For example, during a traffic stop, promptly presenting your driver's license, registration, and proof of insurance upon request demonstrates compliance with lawful requirements. This cooperative gesture can satisfy the officer's immediate needs without compromising your rights. If questions extend beyond these basics, you can then choose to assert your right to remain silent as previously discussed.

At times, an officer may continue to ask questions even after you've asserted your right to remain silent. It's important to remain calm and refrain from responding. Reiterating your position calmly, "As I mentioned, I prefer not to answer any questions," reinforces your stance without escalating the situation. If pressure persists, you might inquire, "Am I free to leave, or am I being detained?" This question can help clarify your status and prompt the officer to articulate any legal basis for continued detention. However, it's also important to be mindful of the context.

Different situations may call for different responses. In high-stress scenarios, such as active crime scenes or when officers are on high alert, exercising additional caution in your interactions is prudent. Reading the environment and adjusting your approach accordingly can enhance your safety and the overall outcome of the encounter.

While you have the absolute right to remain silent, you should understand that officers may rely on available information to assess situations for criminality. If your silence contributes to uncertainty or leaves critical questions unanswered, the officer may feel compelled to investigate further.

Balancing your right to silence with providing sufficient information to allay immediate concerns can sometimes be advantageous. For instance, if an officer is responding to a report that matches your description, and you have a valid explanation that clearly distinguishes you from the suspect, briefly conveying this information may resolve the matter swiftly. In such cases, offering a concise statement like, "I believe there may be a misunderstanding; I am returning from work and have not been in that area," can clarify the situation without delving into unnecessary details.

Ultimately, the decision of how much to say rests with you. Weighing the potential benefits of minimal, non-incriminating disclosure against the risks of self-incrimination is a personal judgment call. Being informed about your rights and the possible consequences of your choices equips you to make decisions that align with your best interests, and bearing in mind how your actions may reflect in a courtroom should always be at the forefront of your thoughts. Different situations may require varying degrees of silence, and exercising proportionate discretion in these situations cannot be understated.

The Miranda Warning

Originating from a landmark Supreme Court decision, the Miranda Warning is a procedural safeguard designed to ensure that individuals are aware of their Fifth Amendment rights against self-incrimination and their Sixth Amendment right to counsel anytime they are questioned while they are arrested.

The Miranda Warning was established in the 1966 Supreme Court case of Miranda v. Arizona. In the case, Ernesto Miranda was arrested in Phoenix, Arizona, on suspicion of kidnapping and rape. After two hours of police interrogation, Miranda confessed to the crimes and signed a written statement without being informed of his right to remain silent or his right to an attorney. At trial, his confession was used as the primary evidence against him, leading to his conviction. Miranda appealed, arguing that his Fifth Amendment rights had been violated because he was not aware that he could refuse to answer questions or request legal counsel.

The Supreme Court agreed with Miranda, holding that the Fifth Amendment's protection against self-incrimination extends to individuals in police custody and that procedural safeguards are necessary to secure this right. The Court established that prior to any custodial interrogation, law enforcement officers must inform the individual of certain rights: the right to remain silent, that anything said can be used against them in court, the right to consult with an attorney, and if they are unable to afford an attorney, the right to have one appointed. These warnings are now universally known as the Miranda Rights or Miranda Warning.

The purpose of the Miranda Warning is to ensure that

any statements made during a custodial interrogation are the product of a voluntary, knowing, and intelligent waiver of rights. The Court recognized that the inherently coercive nature of police interrogations could undermine an individual's ability to exercise their constitutional protections without proper notification. By requiring officers to inform individuals of their rights, the Miranda decision aimed to prevent compelled self-incrimination and to preserve the fairness and integrity of the criminal justice system.

The obligation for law enforcement to administer the Miranda Warning arises specifically during "custodial interrogation." This term encompasses two key components: custody and interrogation.

Custody refers to situations where an individual's freedom of movement is restrained to a degree associated with formal arrest. Interrogation involves direct questioning or actions by law enforcement that are reasonably likely to elicit an incriminating response. Custody is not limited to situations where a person is formally arrested. It can also include circumstances where a reasonable person would feel they are not free to leave due to the actions of law enforcement.

Factors such as the location of the encounter, the duration, the presence of physical restraints, and the demeanor of the officers can influence this determination. For example, being handcuffed and placed in a police vehicle would typically constitute custody, whereas a brief roadside stop might not. Interrogation, in the context of Miranda Warnings, extends beyond direct questioning. It includes any words or actions by police officers that they should know are reasonably likely to elicit an incriminating response.

This can involve psychological tactics, deceptive practices, or indirect prompts designed to encourage self-incrimination. The courts have recognized that the coercive environment of custody amplifies the pressure on individuals to speak, necessitating the protective measures of the Miranda Warning.

There are, however, exceptions to the Miranda requirement. One notable exception is the "public safety exception," established in the 1984 Supreme Court case of New York v. Quarles. Under this exception, if officers have an immediate need to protect the public or themselves from imminent danger, they may ask questions without providing the Miranda Warning.

For instance, if a suspect is believed to have hidden a weapon in a public place, officers can inquire about its location to prevent harm. It's important to note that any statements obtained under this exception may still be admissible in court despite the absence of a Miranda Warning.

Another exception involves routine booking questions, such as inquiries about an individual's name, address, date of birth, or other biographical information. These questions are considered administrative and not intended to elicit incriminating responses, so they do not require a Miranda Warning. However, if officers use the guise of routine questioning to gather incriminating evidence, the protections of Miranda may still apply.

Understanding the concept of "waiving" Miranda Rights is also essential. After being informed of your rights, you may choose to waive them and speak with law enforcement. For a waiver to be valid, it must be made voluntarily, knowingly, and intelligently. This means you must fully understand the rights you are relinquishing and the potential consequences of doing so.

Law enforcement officers often ask individuals to sign a waiver form or obtain verbal confirmation that they comprehend their rights and agree to proceed without an attorney. It's critical to recognize the implications of waiving your Miranda Rights. Once waived, any statements you make can be used against you in court.

Officers may employ various strategies to encourage a waiver, such as minimizing the seriousness of the situation, implying that cooperation will lead to leniency, or suggesting that remaining silent will have negative repercussions. It's important to approach such decisions with caution and to consider seeking legal counsel before waiving any rights.

It's also important to understand that if you invoke your right to remain silent, law enforcement may, under certain circumstances, re-initiate questioning after a "significant period" and after providing a fresh Miranda Warning. However, if you request an attorney, interrogation must cease until legal counsel is provided, unless you initiate further communication with the police.

It is important to recognize that a request for an attorney must be direct, clear, and affirmative. For example, in the 1994 Supreme Court case of Davis v. United States, the Court held that the phrase "Maybe I should talk to a lawyer," was not a legitimate request for legal counsel. The Court reasoned that "If the suspect's statement is not an unambiguous or unequivocal request for counsel, the officers have no obligation to stop questioning him."

The distinction between invoking the right to silence and the right to counsel carries different legal consequences and emphasizes the importance of precise communication.

The Miranda Warning does not apply in all interactions

with law enforcement. During non-custodial encounters—where you are free to leave—or brief detainments such as Terry stops, officers are not required to provide the warning, even if they ask incriminating questions. Additionally, spontaneous or voluntary statements made without prompting by officers are admissible in court, regardless of whether a Miranda Warning was given. Therefore, exercising caution in your speech at all times during police interactions is advisable.

Contrary to popular belief, the failure of law enforcement to provide a Miranda Warning when required does not automatically result in the dismissal of charges. Instead, the primary remedy is the exclusion of any statements made without the warning from being used as evidence in court. This is known as the "exclusionary rule." However, there are exceptions where unlawfully obtained statements may still be admissible, such as for impeachment purposes if you testify inconsistently at trial. If an officer fails to read you a Miranda Warning, that does not disqualify any of the other evidence obtained against you, and an officer may conduct a lawful arrest without ever providing a Miranda Warning.

For the average citizen, the practical takeaway is simple: If you find yourself in a situation where you are in police custody and subject to questioning, pay close attention to whether you have been provided the Miranda Warning. If not, you may inquire, "Am I free to leave, or am I under arrest?" This question helps clarify your status.

If you are not free to leave, and officers begin questioning you without providing the warning, you can assert your rights by stating, "I would like to exercise my right to remain silent and request an attorney." Even if the Miranda Warning is provided, consider carefully before choosing to waive your rights.

The stress and pressure of custodial interrogation can impair judgment, and without legal counsel, you may inadvertently make statements that harm your legal position. Remember that law enforcement officers are trained interrogators, skilled in techniques designed to elicit information. Recognizing when the warning is required, how to assert your rights, and the implications of waiving those rights serves as a practical tool for ensuring that your constitutional protections are honored and your statements are not used against you in court.

Compelled Statements and Legal Obligations

Understanding your legal obligations during police encounters involves recognizing the difference between lawful commands and requests that infringe upon constitutional protections. While you must comply with lawful orders, such as producing identification when required by law or following instructions during a traffic stop, you are not obligated to answer questions that delve into potentially incriminating territory.

In some instances, officers may imply that failing to answer questions could lead to negative consequences. They might suggest that cooperation will make the process smoother or that silence could be perceived as suspicious. It's crucial to remember that the Fifth Amendment protects you from being compelled to provide testimony against yourself, and exercising this right cannot legally be used against you in court. The choice to remain silent in the face of potentially incriminating questions is a fundamental constitutional protection, not an admission of guilt.

As the Supreme Court held in the 1979 case of Michigan

v. DeFillippo "while a person may be briefly detained against his will on the basis of reasonable suspicion while pertinent questions are directed to him, the person stopped is not obliged to answer, answers may not be compelled, and refusal to answer furnishes no basis for an arrest." The phrase "answers may not be compelled" means that police officers cannot force you to answer their questions beyond what you are legally obligated to say, however, there are also situations where providing certain information is mandatory due to public safety considerations.

For instance, if you are involved in a traffic accident, state laws typically require you to provide your name, address, vehicle registration, and insurance information to the other party and responding officers. These requirements are designed to facilitate the exchange of necessary information for legal and insurance purposes and do not infringe upon the Fifth Amendment because they are not inherently incriminating. However, even in these scenarios, you are not obligated to provide statements about how the accident occurred or admit fault. You can comply with legal obligations by providing the required information while refraining from discussing the details of the incident without legal counsel. If pressed for such information, you may respond by stating, "I prefer to discuss this matter with my attorney before making any statements."

It's important to note that the privilege against self-incrimination applies only to testimonial evidence, not physical evidence. You can be compelled to provide fingerprints, chemical or DNA samples, or participate in lineups without violating the Fifth Amendment. The rationale is that these forms of evidence are not communicative in nature and do not involve disclosing the contents of your mind.

Courts have grappled with whether forcing an individual to unlock a device violates the Fifth Amendment. Some courts have distinguished between compelling someone to produce a physical act, like providing a fingerprint to unlock a phone, and compelling someone to reveal knowledge, such as a memorized passcode. The latter is more likely to be protected under the Fifth Amendment, as it involves revealing the contents of one's mind. The legal landscape of Fifth Amendment protections continues to flourish and adapt to the demands of modern society to this very day, and technological advancements continue to challenge traditional legal frameworks of these protections.

In all interactions with law enforcement, maintaining a clear understanding of your legal obligations versus your rights against self-incrimination is crucial. Complying with lawful commands, such as providing identification when required, demonstrates respect for the law and can prevent additional complications. Simultaneously, confidently asserting your constitutional rights safeguards you from overreach and preserves the integrity of the legal process.

Preparation and awareness are key. Familiarize yourself with the specific laws in your state regarding identification and other legal obligations during police encounters. Knowing whether your state has "stop-and-identify" statutes and understanding the extent of those laws allows you to respond appropriately. Navigating the balance between compelled answers and legal obligations requires a nuanced understanding of both your duties under the law and your constitutional protections.

By recognizing when you are legally required to provide information and when you have the right to remain silent, you can engage with law enforcement in a manner that respects both your rights and the responsibilities inherent in a lawful society. Clear communication, respectful assertion of your rights, and knowledge of the legal framework equip you to handle police interactions with confidence and integrity.

Chapter Six
Standing Up for Your Rights

Police encounters can be some of the most stressful and confusing moments that a person may face in their life. It's difficult to know what the right course of action is when your instincts are telling you to defend yourself, your privacy, or your dignity. Knowing your rights is essential, but it's equally important to understand how to navigate these encounters safely. When faced with an armed authority figure demanding compliance, the stakes feel impossibly high. In these moments, what you do, and don't do, can make a significant difference in the outcome. While knowing your rights is essential, understanding the practical realities of these situations can help keep you safe

Staying Calm Under Stress:
Lessons from the Daniel Shaver Case

One of the most crucial yet challenging things to do during a police encounter is to stay calm. Staying calm, however, isn't just about controlling your emotions—it's about maintaining clarity of thought, listening carefully, and moving deliberately. This skill can be life-saving. The tragic story of Daniel Shaver serves as an example of how panic, confusion, and fear can be a catalyst for fatal police interactions.

In January 2016, Daniel Shaver, a 26-year-old pest control specialist from Texas, was staying at a La Quinta Inn in Mesa, Arizona. After showing off a legally owned pellet gun he used for his job to two acquaintances in his hotel room, someone reported to the hotel staff that a man was pointing a gun out of a window. The staff called the police, fearing a potential threat.

Responding to the call, six Mesa police officers arrived at the hotel. Body camera footage later revealed the chaotic and distressing nature of the encounter. Officers confronted Shaver in the hallway outside his room. He was unarmed, wearing only basketball shorts and a T-shirt, and appeared visibly frightened. Officer Philip Brailsford, armed with an AR-15 rifle, took the lead.

Shaver was met with a barrage of complex and conflicting commands: he was ordered to lie down, cross his ankles, put his hands up, and then crawl towards the officers. The instructions were shouted rapidly, leaving little room for error. At one point, Shaver, sobbing and pleading for his life, reached towards his waistband—possibly to pull up his slipping shorts. Interpreting this movement as a potential threat, Officer Brailsford fired five shots, killing Shaver instantly. Officer Brailsford was initially charged with second-degree murder and reckless manslaughter, but was later acquitted the following year.

It is clear from the footage of the Shaver incident that he posed no threat to the officers, and the officers acted recklessly to say the least. Not only is it entirely possible to be killed by the police over a simple misunderstanding or an unexpected gesture, but they may never face any repercussions for your death.

The Shaver case highlights the dangers of failing to remain calm and follow instructions precisely. But it also underscores how difficult it is to stay composed when you are terrified and receiving conflicting commands. While officers should be trained to de-escalate such situations, it would be unwise to depend on an officer's willingness and ability to de-escalate a situation, rather than proactively working toward de-escalation on your own.

The main lessons of the Shaver case are as follows:

Listen Carefully: Attempt to focus intently on the officer's commands, even amidst chaos. This is much easier said than done in almost any interaction, however, understanding the intent of a police officer is the first step in determining how you should respond. Listen closely, and let the officer do as much talking as they feel they need to do, and remember that the correct way to challenge police misconduct is through the courts, not on the street

.

Move Deliberately: Avoid sudden or ambiguous movements; if you need to adjust clothing or scratch an itch, politely communicate your intentions clearly before doing so. Avoid placing your hands in your pockets or anywhere the officer cannot plainly see them. You want to avoid doing anything that would allow an officer to say that they were 'in fear of their safety' when interacting with you as this could become an important aspect of the stop if it does end up in court.

Communicate Respectfully: Use calm and clear language to express confusion or fear, such as, "Officer, I'm trying to comply. Please repeat the instructions." Even if you are expressing a disagreement with an officer it is always in your best interest to remain respectful. Never let an officer's bad attitude get the best of you.

While it's crucial to acknowledge that the onus of de-escalation should not rest solely on civilians, and law enforcement agencies must prioritize effective training, the reality is that in the moment, your actions can influence the outcome of an encounter and have potentially life-altering consequences. Remaining calm, emotionally neutral, and compliant will not only help whatever legal troubles might follow a police interaction, but it could very well save your life.

The Psychology of Police Encounters

A sudden flash of blue lights in your rearview mirror, a stern command to pull over, or an unexpected knock on your door can trigger a cascade of emotions like fear, anxiety, and confusion. To properly navigate police interactions, it is essential to delve beyond the surface of legal rights and procedures and explore the psychological dynamics at play. By understanding both your own mindset and that of the police officer, you can better manage your reactions, communicate more effectively, and increase the likelihood of a safe and positive outcome.

Police officers and civilians often approach encounters from vastly different psychological standpoints, each shaped by their experiences, training, and societal influences. Recognizing these differences is the first step toward bridging the gap that can lead to misunderstandings or escalations.

From the officer's perspective, the primary objective is to ensure safety, their own, that of the civilian, and that of the public. This focus on safety is ingrained through rigorous training and reinforced by the inherent risks of the profession. Every traffic stop, pedestrian interaction, or response to a call carries the potential for danger. Officers are taught to maintain control over situations to mitigate these risks. This training emphasizes vigilance, quick assessment of threats, and decisive action when necessary.

This mindset can lead to a heightened state of alertness, sometimes referred to as "hyper-vigilance." Officers are constantly scanning for signs of danger, which can include anything from a quick movement to a subtle shift in tone of voice. While this vigilance is a necessary aspect of their job, it can also result in misinterpretations of innocent behaviors. For example, a nervous reach for a wallet might be perceived as a potential threat. Existing in a constant state of hyper-vigilance can have detrimental effects on a person's long term mental health, leading them to make potentially irrational or overly aggressive decisions.

The culture within law enforcement further shapes an officer's psychological approach. Concepts like the "thin blue line" underscore a perception of officers as the barrier between order and chaos. This can foster a strong sense of duty and camaraderie, but may also contribute to an "us versus them" mentality. In high-crime areas or communities with strained police relations, this mindset can become more pronounced, affecting how officers perceive and interact with civilians.

Officers also operate under significant stress. Long hours, exposure to traumatic events, and the weight of responsibility can take a psychological toll. Stress and fatigue can impair judgment, reduce patience, and increase the likelihood of miscommunication. An officer dealing with these factors may respond more brusquely or be less receptive to explanations, not out of malice but due to the cumulative pressures of the job.

On the other side of the encounter, civilians bring their own psychological baggage. Being stopped or approached by the police can trigger the body's fight-or-flight response. This physiological reaction, rooted in our evolutionary survival mechanisms, can cause increased heart rate, rapid breathing, and heightened anxiety. These symptoms can, in turn, affect behavior, making a person appear nervous, agitated, or uncooperative, even when they intend to comply fully.

Officers are trained to observe and interpret behavior, including signs of nervousness. In their experience, nervousness can sometimes indicate that a person is hiding something—be it contraband, involvement in a crime, or outstanding warrants. However, it's also widely recognized that most people feel nervous during encounters with law enforcement, even when they have done nothing wrong. Courts have grappled with this reality, acknowledging that nervousness alone is not sufficient to establish reasonable suspicion. Nevertheless, when combined with other factors, it can contribute to an officer's decision to investigate further.

In the case of United States v. Beck, the Eighth Circuit Court of Appeals addressed this very issue. The court found that nervousness is of "limited significance" in determining reasonable suspicion because "it is common for most people to exhibit signs of nervousness when confronted by a law enforcement officer." This recognition by the judiciary highlights the importance of considering nervousness in context rather than as a standalone indicator of criminal activity.

Conversely, in Illinois v. Wardlow, the United States Supreme Court held that nervous, evasive behavior could contribute to reasonable suspicion. In this case, the defendant fled upon seeing police officers in a high-crime area, and the Court ruled that such flight was suggestive of wrongdoing. The key distinction here is the combination of nervousness with evasive actions and the context of the environment.

While you cannot eliminate nervousness, you can manage how it manifests and how it is perceived. The goal is not to suppress your natural feelings but to present yourself in a way that minimizes misunderstandings and reduces the likelihood of unnecessary escalation. Here are a few practical strategies to help manage nervousness:

Acknowledge Nervousness: If an officer comments on your demeanor, it's acceptable to say, "Yes, officer, I'm feeling a bit nervous because I've never been in this situation before." Offering a reasonable and practical explanation for your nervousness can be a powerful tool for both dispelling an officer's suspicion of you and defending your innocence in any subsequent court case that may arise from the encounter.

Controlled Breathing: Practice deep breathing techniques to help calm your nerves and reduce physical signs of anxiety. Controlled breathing stimulates the vagus nerve, which activates the parasympathetic nervous system, which is the part of your body responsible for relaxation and rest. This leads to a decrease in heart rate and blood pressure, counteracting the "fight or flight" response initiated by stress. This technique can also lower levels of stress hormones like cortisol, and has been scientifically proven to be an effective technique for dealing with stressful situations.

Positive Affirmations: Remind yourself mentally that staying calm will help you navigate the situation more effectively. Although this may seem vague and somewhat whimsical, the concept of positive affirmations is rooted in cognitive behavioral therapy and serves as a practical and accessible tool for managing stress and promoting emotional well-being. Regularly practicing positive affirmations can help reprogram the subconscious mind. By replacing negative self-talk with positive statements, affirmations can reduce anxiety and promote a calmer mental state. Much like controlled breathing techniques, positive affirmations have been shown to lower cortisol levels and help alleviate physical symptoms of stress, such as increased heart rate and muscle tension.

It is important to bear in mind that maintaining calm during emotionally taxing situations is a skill that can be developed through practicing these techniques, along with a litany of other mindfulness exercises. Along with building an understanding of your constitutional rights, you should also devote time and effort to building a strong mind that is capable of recalling and effectively asserting those rights. While nervousness does tend to play a major role during police interactions, it is not the only psychological element that citizens should consider.

There's also the perceived power imbalance. Police officers wield significant authority, backed by the legal system and, if necessary, the use of force. This imbalance can make civilians feel vulnerable or powerless, intensifying feelings of fear or resentment. These emotions can cloud judgment, leading to actions or words that may unintentionally escalate the situation.

Moreover, societal factors play a role in shaping civilians' perceptions of police encounters. Media reports of police misconduct, personal experiences, or stories from friends and family can influence how one approaches an interaction with law enforcement. For some, especially individuals from marginalized communities, there may be a deep-seated mistrust or fear of police based on historical or ongoing issues of bias and discrimination.

Understanding these psychological underpinnings is crucial for navigating police encounters effectively. By recognizing the factors influencing both parties, you can adopt strategies to manage your own reactions and help de-escalate potential tensions.

It's also essential to be aware of your legal rights during a police encounter, but equally important is how you assert them. You have the right to remain silent and the right to refuse consent to a search in many situations. However, the manner in which you assert these rights can influence the officer's perception of your cooperation. Stating, "Officer, I prefer not to answer any questions without an attorney present," is a respectful way to assert your rights without appearing confrontational.

Asserting your rights firmly yet politely can help protect you legally while minimizing the risk of escalating the encounter. Avoiding aggressive or sarcastic tones is crucial. Remember, the goal is to get through the interaction safely and address any grievances later through appropriate legal channels.

Societal issues such as implicit bias and racial profiling cannot be ignored when discussing the psychology of police encounters. While these systemic problems require broad policy changes and community efforts to address, being aware of them can inform your approach during an interaction. Recognizing that an officer may hold unconscious biases allows you to tailor your behavior in ways that might mitigate negative perceptions.

For instance, individuals who feel they may be unfairly targeted can focus on maintaining an extra level of composure and clarity in communication. While it's unjust that this burden falls heavier on some than others, understanding the reality can help you navigate the situation more safely.

Preparation can also play a significant role in managing police encounters. Just as officers train for various scenarios, civilians can benefit from mental rehearsal. Educating yourself on what to expect during a traffic stop or pedestrian encounter can reduce uncertainty and anxiety. Familiarize yourself with standard procedures and think through how you would respond in different situations.

Visualization techniques can be helpful. Imagine yourself in a police encounter, practicing how you would respond to requests, how you would communicate, and how you would manage your emotions. This mental preparation can make your responses more automatic and controlled when faced with the real situation.

Understanding the psychology of police encounters is a multifaceted endeavor that involves recognizing the fears, motivations, and perceptions of both officers and civilians. By approaching these interactions with empathy, respect, and informed awareness, you can significantly influence the outcome. Remember that while you cannot control the officer's behavior, you have control over your own responses.

Maintaining composure, communicating effectively, and asserting your rights respectfully are all strategies within your power. These approaches not only help protect your legal interests but also contribute to a safer environment for everyone involved. Empowered with this knowledge, you can navigate police encounters with greater confidence and poise, transforming a potentially stressful situation into one that is manageable and, hopefully, uneventful.

When and How to Comply

Navigating interactions with law enforcement requires a delicate balance between asserting your legal rights and ensuring your personal safety. Understanding when and how to comply with police commands is a crucial aspect of this balance. While the Constitution provides robust protections against unreasonable searches and seizures, the practical realities of a police encounter often necessitate a thoughtful approach to compliance.

In the moment of an encounter, the distinction between lawful and unlawful commands may not always be clear. Police officers are vested with significant authority to maintain public safety, but they are also bound by legal constraints. However, challenging an officer's command on the spot can lead to immediate consequences, including arrest or the use of force. It's important to recognize that the street is not the ideal forum for legal debates; courts exist precisely to adjudicate disputes over rights and authority. Therefore, understanding the appropriate times to comply, and how to do so effectively, can help you avoid unnecessary risks while preserving your ability to seek redress later.

When an officer issues a command, your immediate assessment should focus on safety, for both yourself and the officer. If the command involves actions like keeping your hands visible, stepping out of your vehicle, or providing identification, it's generally advisable to comply promptly. These requests are standard procedures aimed at ensuring that the encounter proceeds without incident. Refusal or hesitation in these situations may be interpreted as non-compliance or even as a potential threat, which could escalate tensions.

Consider a routine traffic stop as an example. If an officer asks you to produce your driver's license and registration, providing these documents without delay can help keep the interaction brief and uneventful. If you need to reach into a glove compartment or bag to retrieve them, it's prudent to inform the officer of your actions beforehand. A simple statement like, "My registration is in the glove compartment; may I reach for it?" can alleviate any concerns the officer might have about sudden movements.

There may be instances where an officer's command appears to infringe upon your rights. For example, you might be asked to consent to a search of your vehicle or person without a clear justification. The Fourth Amendment protects you against unreasonable searches and seizures, meaning that, in many cases, you have the right to refuse consent to a search. However, it's essential to assert this right calmly and respectfully. You might say, "Officer, I do not consent to any searches." This statement clearly communicates your position without adopting a confrontational tone.

It's important to note that refusing consent does not guarantee that a search won't occur. Officers may proceed if they believe they have probable cause or under certain exigent circumstances. If an officer insists on conducting a search despite your refusal, it's generally safer to allow the search to proceed without physical resistance. You can document the encounter mentally or, if permissible and safe, record it using your phone. Any disputes over the legality of the search can be addressed later in court.

During an encounter, you might also be subjected to questioning that feels intrusive or accusatory. The Fifth Amendment grants you the right against self-incrimination, meaning you are not obligated to answer questions that could incriminate you. If you choose to exercise this right, it's advisable to do so explicitly and politely. You could say, "I prefer not to answer any questions without an attorney present." Again, the manner in which you assert your rights can influence the tone of the interaction.

Understanding that officers are legally permitted to use certain deceptive tactics is also crucial. They may imply that cooperating will benefit you or suggest that refusing a request could have negative consequences. While these statements can be intimidating, it's important to remain steadfast yet courteous in your responses. Remember that any promises or threats made during the encounter may not hold legal weight, and decisions about charges or leniency are typically made by prosecutors and judges, not officers on the scene.

In situations where you believe an officer is issuing an unlawful command, such as demanding entry into your home without a warrant or exigent circumstances, the safest course of action is often to express your refusal calmly and state your understanding of your rights. For example, you might say, "Officer, I do not consent to entry without a warrant." If the officer persists, it's generally safer to step aside and allow them to proceed rather than physically blocking their way. Any legal violations can be challenged later with the assistance of legal counsel.

Communication plays a pivotal role in these encounters. Keeping your tone respectful and your language clear can help de-escalate potential tensions. Avoid using aggressive or sarcastic remarks, as these can be misconstrued or may exacerbate the situation. If you feel that the officer is not listening or is becoming agitated, maintaining your composure becomes even more critical. Deep breathing and measured speech can aid in keeping the interaction as calm as possible.

It's also beneficial to be aware of your body language. Nonverbal cues can significantly impact how an officer perceives you. Standing upright with a relaxed posture, maintaining appropriate eye contact, and keeping your hands visible can convey cooperation. Avoid sudden movements, and if you need to reach for something, communicate your intentions first.

In the digital age, many people consider recording police encounters. While recording can provide valuable documentation, it's important to understand the laws in your jurisdiction regarding such recordings. Some states require dual-party consent for audio recordings, while others allow for public recordings of officers performing their duties. If you choose to record, do so openly and inform the officer by saying something like, "Officer, I am informing you that I will be recording this interaction for my records." Ensure that recording does not interfere with the officer's duties or pose a safety risk.

Throughout the encounter, keeping the ultimate goal in mind is essential: to conclude the interaction safely while preserving your rights. This may require a degree of patience and restraint, especially if you feel that your rights are being challenged. Remember that the side of the road is not the place to adjudicate legal disputes. Reacting impulsively or antagonistically can lead to immediate negative consequences that may outweigh any short-term satisfaction from asserting a point.

After the encounter has concluded, you have the opportunity to address any grievances through proper legal channels. If you believe that your rights were violated, consult with an attorney who can advise you on the appropriate steps to take. This might include filing a complaint with the police department's internal affairs division, pursuing civil litigation, or seeking other forms of redress.

Knowing when and how to comply with police commands involves a careful assessment of the situation, a clear understanding of your rights, and a strategic approach to communication and behavior. By prioritizing safety and employing thoughtful compliance, you can navigate police encounters more effectively, reducing the risk of escalation while preserving your ability to address any issues through the legal system later.

The Reality of Police Deception

In the intricate dance of a police encounter, one factor often overlooked by citizens is the role of deception. It's a disconcerting truth that law enforcement officers are legally permitted to employ deceptive tactics during interactions and investigations. This reality can have profound implications for your rights and the decisions you make when facing police questioning or requests. Understanding the extent and limitations of police deception is essential for navigating these encounters wisely and safeguarding your legal protections.

At first glance, the idea that officers can lie to you may seem contrary to the pursuit of justice. We are taught from a young age to trust the police as upholders of the law and paragons of honesty. However, the legal system recognizes deception as a legitimate tool in the arsenal of law enforcement, intended to elicit information, confessions, or compliance that might not be forthcoming through straightforward means.

The courts have long upheld the permissibility of police deception in certain contexts. The Supreme Court has ruled that the use of trickery or misrepresentation by law enforcement does not necessarily violate the Constitution, particularly the Fifth Amendment's protection against self-incrimination. In the landmark 1989 case of Frazier v. Cupp, the Court held that the fact that an officer lied to a suspect about a co-defendant's confession did not make the suspect's subsequent confession involuntary. This and other rulings have established a legal framework wherein deception is considered acceptable, provided it does not induce an involuntary or coerced confession.

One common form of police deception involves misrepresenting the evidence against you. An officer might claim to have surveillance footage, eyewitness testimony, or forensic proof that doesn't actually exist. The goal is to make you believe that denial is futile and that cooperation is your best option. For example, during an interrogation, an officer might say, "We found your fingerprints at the scene," even if no such evidence exists. This tactic is designed to compel you to admit involvement out of a sense of inevitability.

Another deceptive practice is the suggestion of leniency in exchange for cooperation. Officers may imply that confessing or providing information will result in lesser charges or more favorable treatment. They might say, "Help us out, and we'll put in a good word with the prosecutor," or "Things will go easier for you if you tell the truth now." It's important to understand that police officers do not have the authority to grant leniency; decisions about charges and sentencing rest with prosecutors and judges. Relying on such promises can lead you to relinquish rights without any guaranteed benefit. Never trust any deals, compromises, or offers that members of law enforcement make to you and always consult an attorney before discussing anything related to your case with an officer.

Officers may also use deception to obtain consent for searches. They might suggest that refusing a search would be pointless or that compliance could prevent further inconvenience. Phrases like "If you have nothing to hide, you won't mind if we take a quick look" are designed to make refusal seem suspicious or futile. In reality, you have the constitutional right to refuse consent to a search, even if it's lawful and you are legally obligated to comply. Succumbing to this subtle pressure can result in the discovery of evidence that might not have been lawfully obtained otherwise.

The use of deception isn't limited to interrogations or requests for consent. During street encounters, officers might misrepresent the reason for a stop or suggest that non-compliance could lead to immediate negative consequences. For instance, an officer might imply that failing to answer questions could result in arrest, even if they lack sufficient grounds to detain you. These tactics exploit the average citizen's uncertainty about legal procedures and rights.

It should be noted that an officer's ability to gain consent through deception does not apply to lying about a warrant. In the 1968 case of Bumper v. North Carolina, the Supreme Court held that "Orderly submission to law enforcement officers who, in effect, represented to the defendant that they had the authority to enter and search the house, against his will if necessary, was not such consent as constituted an understanding, intentional and voluntary waiver by the defendant of his fundamental rights under the Fourth Amendment to the Constitution." In other words, submitting to law enforcement officers who lie about having a warrant to search does not qualify as a consent search.

Understanding that officers may employ deception underscores the importance of being cautious with your words and actions during an encounter. As discussed in chapter five, the Fifth Amendment grants you the right to remain silent to avoid self-incrimination. You are not obligated to answer questions that could incriminate you, and exercising this right cannot legally be used against you in court. However, it's crucial to assert this right explicitly and respectfully. Simply remaining silent without stating your intent may lead to confusion or additional pressure. A clear statement like "I choose to remain silent" or "I would like to speak with an attorney before answering any questions" communicates your position firmly yet politely.

Similarly, as mentioned in chapter two, the Fourth Amendment protects you against unreasonable searches and seizures. Unless an officer has probable cause, a warrant, or certain exigent circumstances, you are under no obligation to consent to a search of your person, vehicle, or property. If you wish to refuse a search, it's advisable to do so verbally and calmly. Saying "I do not consent to a search" is sufficient. Remember that physical resistance is never advisable, as it can lead to charges of obstruction or worse. Even if an officer proceeds with a search after you have refused consent, it is much safer and more prudent to challenge their actions in court, not on the street.

It's also important to be aware that your demeanor and the way you communicate can influence the officer's response. While you may feel frustration or indignation upon realizing that deception is being used, reacting with hostility can escalate the situation. Maintaining composure and speaking in a measured tone can help de-escalate potential tensions. Keep in mind that officers are often trained to interpret certain behaviors or attitudes as signs of guilt or aggression, which can justify further investigative actions in their eyes.

In some cases, officers may attempt to build rapport as a means of eliciting information. They might engage in casual conversation, express sympathy, or share personal anecdotes to encourage you to open up. While these approaches may feel less confrontational, they are nonetheless strategic. Anything you say can be used against you, even if it seems innocuous at the time. Being mindful of this can help you avoid inadvertently sharing information that could be detrimental to your interests.

The legal acceptance of police deception places a greater burden on citizens to be informed and vigilant. It's not about fostering distrust but about empowering yourself with knowledge. Recognizing the potential for deception allows you to navigate encounters more effectively, making informed decisions rather than reactive ones. It also highlights the importance of consulting with an attorney before making statements or decisions that could have legal ramifications.

It's worth acknowledging that the use of deception by law enforcement is a contentious issue, and debates continue about its ethical implications and effectiveness. Some argue that it undermines public trust and can lead to false confessions, particularly among vulnerable populations. Proponents contend that it is a necessary tool for combating crime in a world where individuals may not be forthcoming with the truth. Regardless of where one stands on the issue, the reality remains that deception is a legally sanctioned tactic, and being aware of it is essential for protecting oneself.

The reality of police deception is a critical aspect of law enforcement interactions that every citizen should understand. By recognizing that officers may use misleading statements or tactics, you can better protect your rights and make informed decisions during encounters. Remember to exercise your right to remain silent, refuse consent to unwarranted searches, and request legal counsel when appropriate. Doing so respectfully and calmly can help you navigate these challenging situations while minimizing the risk of escalation. Knowledge is your most valuable asset in these circumstances.

Reality Check: The Prevalence of Uneventful Police Encounters

Amidst the headlines and social media narratives that often highlight confrontations between civilians and law enforcement, it's easy to develop a skewed perception of police encounters.

High-profile cases involving excessive force or civil rights violations capture our attention and, understandably, provoke concern and fear. However, it's important to recognize that these incidents, while significant and deserving of scrutiny, are not representative of the majority of interactions between police officers and the public. In reality, countless police encounters occur daily without incident, resolving smoothly and professionally. Understanding this context can provide a balanced perspective, reduce anxiety, and help you approach potential interactions with law enforcement more confidently and pragmatically.

Every day across the United States, millions of people engage with police officers in various capacities—traffic stops, community events, calls for assistance, or casual conversations. The vast majority of these interactions are routine and uneventful. Officers conduct their duties respectfully and efficiently, and citizens comply with reasonable requests, resulting in a peaceful conclusion. These positive or neutral encounters rarely make the news but are integral to the fabric of community policing and public safety.

Consider the statistics: according to data collected by the Bureau of Justice Statistics, tens of millions of face-to-face contacts occur annually between police and the public. These include everything from traffic stops and investigative detentions to emergency responses and community outreach programs. The overwhelming majority of these contacts do not result in the use of force or complaints of misconduct. This isn't to diminish the significance of problematic incidents but to highlight that they are exceptions rather than the rule.

Understanding that most police interactions are uneventful can help alleviate some of the apprehension you might feel when encountering law enforcement. Recognizing this reality allows you to approach such situations with a mindset geared toward cooperation and resolution rather than fear and defensiveness. This perspective doesn't negate the importance of knowing your rights or being prepared to handle potential issues but provides a more grounded foundation from which to navigate these encounters.

Moreover, many officers enter the profession with a genuine desire to serve their communities. They perform a challenging job that often involves mitigating conflicts, assisting those in distress, and maintaining public order. Acknowledging the human aspect of law enforcement can foster a mutual sense of respect and understanding. When both parties approach an interaction with civility and openness, the likelihood of a positive outcome increases significantly.

This isn't to say that systemic issues within law enforcement don't exist or that all officers conduct themselves appropriately. There are legitimate concerns about accountability, bias, and use of force that require ongoing attention and reform. Being aware of these issues is important, but it's equally crucial not to let them overshadow the reality that many officers are committed to ethical and professional conduct.

From a practical standpoint, approaching police interactions with a balanced perspective can benefit you directly. If you enter an encounter expecting conflict, your body language, tone, and responses may reflect that anticipation, potentially influencing the officer's reactions. On the other hand, if you remain calm and composed, you're more likely to facilitate a cooperative exchange.

It's also helpful to remember that officers are human beings who may be influenced by their own experiences, stresses, and perceptions. They may appreciate and respond positively to courteous behavior just as anyone else would. Small gestures like saying "good morning" or "thank you" can set a positive tone. While you should always be mindful of your rights, integrating basic politeness doesn't compromise your legal protections and can enhance the interaction.

It's also beneficial to recognize that police officers often deal with stressful and unpredictable situations. They may be coming from a high-pressure call or managing personal stressors. While it's not your responsibility to manage their emotional state, empathy can guide you toward responses that de-escalate rather than exacerbate tension. Patience and understanding can go a long way in fostering a peaceful resolution.

In the event that an interaction does become challenging, remembering that most encounters are resolved without incident can provide reassurance. It reinforces the idea that difficulties are not inevitable and that you have agency in influencing the outcome. Staying focused on constructive communication and adherence to lawful instructions enhances your ability to navigate the situation effectively.

After the interaction, reflecting on the experience can be valuable. If the encounter was positive, acknowledging that can reinforce your confidence in handling future situations. If you had concerns or felt uncomfortable, considering what factors contributed to that feeling can help you prepare differently next time. In cases where you believe misconduct occurred, knowing that such incidents are exceptions supports the decision to address them through proper channels without generalizing all law enforcement negatively.

Recognizing the prevalence of uneventful police interactions provides a more balanced and realistic understanding of the nature of law enforcement encounters. This perspective doesn't ignore the existence of problematic incidents or the need for systemic improvements but offers a grounded context that can reduce unnecessary fear and promote constructive engagement. By approaching potential encounters with awareness, composure, and a focus on effective communication, you empower yourself to navigate them successfully. Knowledge of your rights remains essential, but coupling that knowledge with a pragmatic appreciation of everyday realities enhances your ability to protect those rights while ensuring your safety and peace of mind.

Empowerment comes from knowledge and preparation. By educating yourself about your rights and the practical realities of police encounters, you position yourself to navigate these challenging moments more effectively. Remember that your primary goal is to ensure your safety while preserving your legal protections. Stay calm, be respectful, and exercise your rights thoughtfully. In doing so, you not only protect yourself but also contribute to a more constructive relationship between law enforcement and the community.

Although many of the principles discussed in this chapter can be difficult to actually put into practice in the midst of the chaos and emotional distress police encounters can induce, the following three chapters seek to provide practical advice on common scenarios you may face when interacting with the police using the concepts we discussed in previous chapters. These chapters should serve as a quick reference guide and will contain much of the same information we have already discussed, but framed in a more practical, condensed, and digestible format.

Chapter Seven
Encountering Police in Public

In the context of police interactions, a public space is an area that is generally open and accessible to everyone without requiring permission. Examples include sidewalks, streets, parks, plazas, shopping malls, and other areas where the public is allowed to move freely. Police officers have more leeway to approach and interact with individuals in public spaces because these areas do not carry the same expectation of privacy as private property. For example, if you are standing on a public sidewalk, an officer can legally approach and ask you questions without any specific justification. In a public space, you also do not have the same protections against searches and seizures as you would on private property, like your home or an enclosed backyard.

When can the police stop you in public?

Anytime the police reasonably suspect that you have or are going to commit a crime they can stop you. It is important to bear in mind that innocent behavior can be considered suspicious in certain circumstances, and there are situations where innocent people can be briefly detained by the police while they conduct an investigation or ensure the safety of the public. Police officers are granted the authority to stop individuals under specific circumstances, primarily based on the legal concept of "reasonable suspicion."

Reasonable Suspicion Defined: Established by the Supreme Court in the 1968 case of Terry v. Ohio, reasonable suspicion allows an officer to briefly detain a person if there are specific and articulable facts suggesting that the individual is involved in criminal activity. Examples include behaviors such as looking into car windows late at night in a high-crime area, matching the description of a suspect, or acting in a way that suggests you may be engaged in illegal activity.

A good rule of thumb is that anytime an officer orders you to "stop", you should immediately comply. Whether or not an officer can lawfully order you to stop hinges on whether or not the officer had met the reasonable suspicion standard at the time they issued the order, and considering that officers are under no legal obligation to tell you the truth about why you are being stopped, they may be operating on information that you are not aware of that lawfully justifies their actions.

For instance, an officer might stop an individual who matches the description of a recent bank robber. The officer might begin by engaging in a consensual encounter with the individual and ask for the individual's name. If the individual refuses to provide their name the officer may then choose to force them to identify themselves without revealing that they are suspected to be a wanted bank robber. It may be in the officer's best interest to avoid revealing the true nature of the stop in an effort to preserve the safety of everyone involved, along with any evidence that may be at risk of destruction.

Now imagine the bank robber was an average citizen who merely fit the description of the suspect, but wasn't actually involved in a bank robbery at all. From their perspective it would be reasonable to assume that the officer was acting irrationally or committing misconduct by demanding to see their identification and refusing to justify their actions. In both scenarios, whether the stopped suspect was a bank robber or just an unfortunately dressed citizen, a lawful nonconsensual encounter took place and no constitutional violations occurred.

What may initially appear to be an illegal stop may later be revealed to be completely justified, so it is vitally important to have all the facts before taking any action during a police encounter. Complying to questionable demands from an officer is sometimes necessary to preserve your freedom and build your case against any officer who you believe may be engaging in misconduct. Disobeying an officer's orders, regardless of whether or not they are lawful, will almost certainly result in being arrested, but it can also be a catalyst for an expensive, time consuming, and emotionally burdening criminal charge. While there are certainly times where advocating for your freedom or expressing dissent for the actions of the officers involved can be beneficial, it is vitally important to exercise discretion during police interactions.

If an officer orders you to "stop" or otherwise expresses that you are not free to leave then you are considered detained and the officer believes they have reasonable suspicion to stop you. Whether or not the officer actually has reasonable suspicion to stop you is a matter that will be dealt with later in court, and you should always comply with an officer's order to stop regardless of your interpretation of the legality of the stop. If an officer stops you, stay calm and ask, "Am I free to leave?" If the officer says yes, then you should leave immediately. If the officer tells you that you are not free to leave then an appropriate response might be "Officer, I am willing to comply with my legal obligations, but I would like to remain silent without my attorney present. Please let me know when I am free to go."

Quick Tip: If you have a friend or family member still involved in an interaction you have been told to leave, then it might be best to find a safe location and try to document as much of the interaction as possible on their behalf. Valuable insights often come from evidence collected by external sources, and any information you capture could become an asset to the court proceedings.

There may be an instance where you, as a citizen, must interact with a member of law enforcement who doesn't fully understand how reasonable suspicion works, and it is vitally important to bear in mind how your behavior may translate to a courtroom and remain as compliant as possible. You never know what information an officer might possess to justify their actions, and, as mentioned before, police officers are under no legal obligation to tell you what justification they have for satisfying reasonable suspicion or probable cause.

What may appear to be an officer who doesn't understand

reasonable suspicion could turn out to be an officer who intentionally withheld certain facts from you. It is always best to assume that an officer who has stopped you has fulfilled the standards of reasonable suspicion even if you think they haven't, and, despite the lack of legal obligation to reply, it is never a bad idea to ask the officer why you are being stopped.

If you can convince an officer to articulate their reasonable suspicion while you are recording them or their body camera is rolling then it will be difficult for them to dispute their account later in court, but most officers who commit acts of misconduct understand the implications of elaborating on their conduct and will likely refuse to answer. There are so many unique variables and highly specific circumstances involved in determining the legitimacy of reasonable suspicion that it would be reckless to assume that any single citizen could make such an analysis with any degree of accuracy, and this is why each instance is considered on a case-by-case basis.

When can the police ask for ID?

In public, whether you are required to provide identification depends on where you are and the nature of the encounter. If you are in a state with a "stop-and-identify" law and an officer asks for your identifying information during a lawful stop, you must provide it. The following graphic depicts which states have adopted stop and identify statutes. If you are in one of these states you must identify yourself to officers if they have stopped you based on reasonable suspicion.

It should be noted that not all stop and identify statutes are the same, and some may have additional requirements beyond simply identifying yourself. For example, the language of New Hampshire's stop and ID statute does not establish a legal requirement to provide documentation of identity, or even a requirement to respond at all, and police officers in New Hampshire are not authorized to arrest citizens for failing to provide identification. Conversely, Colorado's stop and ID statute requires that the person stopped provide their name, address, physical ID, and an explanation of their actions.

Stop-and-Identify States

Each state may have their own unique requirements, and it would be advisable to become familiar with your specific state's stop and ID laws. As mentioned in chapter three, some states that don't have stop-and-identify laws may still charge you with obstruction, or a similar crime, if you refuse to identify yourself

When can the police search you?

There are several situations where the police could search you while you're in public, but an officer's authority to search is subject to strict constitutional limitations. A search is essentially any action by a police officer that involves examining your body, your clothing, or your belongings for evidence of illegal activity. Under the Fourth Amendment, officers are generally required to have a warrant to conduct a search. However, there are important exceptions that allow warrantless searches, each with specific rules and limitations.

Consent Searches: A consent search occurs when you voluntarily agree to let an officer search you or your belongings. Officers are not required to have reasonable suspicion or probable cause if you give consent, which is why they often ask, "Do you mind if I take a look?" or "Can I search you?" You have the right to refuse consent to search. If an officer asks for your permission, you can politely say, "No, I do not consent to any searches." Refusing consent does not give the officer a legal basis to search you. It is your right to deny a search, and it cannot be used as evidence of wrongdoing.

Terry Frisk: A Terry frisk is a limited pat-down of your outer clothing to check for weapons. This type of search is only justified if the officer has reasonable suspicion that you are armed and pose a danger, and the officer conducting the frisk cannot enter your pocket unless they detect a weapon or contraband by "plain feel." Officers are not required to justify their decision to conduct a Terry frisk to the citizen they are searching so it is important to comply with this request regardless of whether you believe the search is lawful or not.

Search Incident to Arrest: If an officer lawfully arrests you, they can search you and the immediate area within your control without a warrant. This type of search is called a search incident to arrest. It is justified by the need to protect officer safety and prevent the destruction of evidence. The search is limited to your person and the area immediately around you, such as your pockets or a bag you are carrying, and must be directly related to the arrest.

Exigent Circumstances: Exigent circumstances allow officers to conduct a search without a warrant if there is an urgent need to act, such as a threat to public safety or the risk of evidence being destroyed. This exception justifies immediate action because waiting for a warrant would be impractical and could compromise the safety of others or the integrity of evidence. If an officer believes someone is in danger, they can act immediately to address the situation. For example, if an officer hears screams for help from a public restroom, they can enter without waiting for a warrant. Likewise, if officers reasonably believe that evidence is being destroyed, they may search without a warrant. For instance, if they see someone attempting to flush drugs down a public restroom toilet, they can intervene and search without delay.

If an officer asks to search you or your belongings, you have the right to refuse unless they have reasonable suspicion, probable cause, or are arresting you. Physically resisting a search, even if it is illegal, can escalate the situation and lead to further legal problems, including charges of resisting arrest. Instead, calmly make it clear that you do not consent and comply physically if the officer proceeds. You can later challenge the search in court. If you believe a search was conducted unlawfully, try to remember details like the officer's name, badge number, location, and the nature of the interaction. If possible, record the encounter without interfering, as this may serve as evidence if you choose to challenge the search later.

Can you record your encounter?

Recording your interactions with the police can be one of the most effective ways to protect yourself from police misconduct and create an accurate record of the encounter. Thanks to smartphones, most people now have the capability to quickly and easily record video or audio of situations that unfold around them, including interactions with law enforcement. The right to record police is an important tool for accountability and transparency, and it is protected under the First Amendment. However, there are limitations and best practices you should be aware of to ensure that your recording is legal and that you stay safe while doing so.

The right to record does not give you the right to interfere with police duties. Interference includes actions that make it difficult for the officer to do their job, such as getting too close to the officer during an arrest, blocking their path, or speaking loudly while they are trying to communicate with someone else.

You also cannot record in areas where you are not legally allowed to be. For example, if an officer enters private property, you do not have the right to follow them into that space to continue recording. It is also important to be mindful of the wiretap laws in your state. Some states have "two-party consent" laws, which means that all parties being recorded must consent to the recording. However, most courts have held that these laws do not apply to public officials, including police officers, performing their duties in public places.

Courts have generally upheld that there is no reasonable expectation of privacy for officers performing their duties in public, and therefore audio recording them is permitted. However, in some states, two-party consent laws have been cited by police, leading to potential legal disputes. If you are in a state with two-party consent laws and you are recording an officer in a public park, you are likely protected under the First Amendment. However, if the officer insists that you cannot record, it may be best to comply and seek legal assistance afterward to avoid escalation.

Quick Tip: To protect your footage from being deleted or confiscated, consider using a livestreaming app, like Twitch or YouTube, so that the recording is immediately backed up online. This way, even if your phone is taken, the footage is saved in a remote location that is inaccessible to the police.

Can the police take your phone or other devices?

Your phone is likely one of your most personal possessions, storing sensitive information, communications, photos, and potentially evidence. The Fourth Amendment protects individuals against unreasonable searches and seizures, and this extends to electronic devices like your phone. However, there are situations where law enforcement may lawfully seize your phone, and it's crucial to understand these circumstances and what rights you have when dealing with police in public.

As a general rule, police officers need a warrant to take and search your phone. The Fourth Amendment requires that searches and seizures must be reasonable, and obtaining a warrant from a judge is a key component of ensuring that reasonableness. The Supreme Court has ruled that police officers must obtain a warrant to search a cell phone, even if the phone was taken incident to an arrest. So even if an officer confiscates your phone, they must still obtain a warrant in order to search the contents of the phone.

Although a warrant is generally required to seize or search a phone, the exceptions we discussed earlier in this chapter, and more in-depth in chapter four, would apply to this situation as well. For example, if police officers see you actively deleting incriminating messages on your phone, they can take your phone immediately to prevent data loss. This would be a lawful seizure under the exigent circumstances exception. However, they still need a warrant to access the data stored on the phone.

If you find yourself in a situation where an officer wants to search or seize your phone you might consider saying "I do not consent to any searches or seizures of my phone." Even if the officer takes your phone, stating your non-consent helps protect your rights and can be useful in challenging the seizure later in court.

Are the police required to identify themselves?

In almost every interaction with law enforcement you will want to know who you are dealing with, especially if the interaction feels tense or is escalating. Whether a police officer is required to identify themselves often depends on the situation, the officer's role, and specific state laws or department policies. Most police departments have policies requiring uniformed officers to identify themselves when interacting with the public. This generally includes providing their name and badge number if requested, and these policies are designed to promote accountability and transparency within the department.

The reality is that these policies are created and governed by the respective police department, and it is up to the department to decide whether or not to create or enforce these policies. In most states, police officers are under no legal obligation to identify themselves and they will likely face no real repercussions for refusing to do so, especially if you fail to file a complaint after their refusal.

It is worth noting that there is a growing trend among states to adopt legislation that does force officers to identify themselves when they interact with citizens. States like Illinois, Colorado, and Connecticut have passed laws that require police officers to identify themselves in some form or another upon request, with some states even requiring the officers to identify themselves without an explicit request from a citizen. Although it is worth checking to see if you live in one of the few states that have laws requiring police to identify themselves, for most of the country, whether or not a police officer identifies themselves is a matter of policy, not law, and there are no explicit constitutional protections that guarantee a citizen the right to know an officer's name.

Can you request a supervisor?

Requesting to speak to a police supervisor during an interaction with law enforcement can help de-escalate a tense situation, ensure accountability, or provide clarity if you believe an officer is acting improperly, however, much like requesting an officer's identity, there is no absolute legal requirement for officers to fulfill your request for a supervisor. Although almost every police department in the country has policies that encourage officers to summon a supervisor if requested, officers are not legally required to do so, and it is up to the department to decide how to punish officers who do not obey its policies. It should also be noted that there may be other circumstances that prevent a supervisor from being on the scene, such as a lack of staffing at the department or a more demanding emergency taking place.

Keep in mind that the goal of requesting a supervisor is to either clarify the situation or address concerns. Aggressive language or behavior may make officers less inclined to accommodate your request. If you feel that requesting a supervisor is warranted, you might consider politely saying, "Respectfully officer, I think we are having a miscommunication. I would like to speak to your supervisor, please." You do not have to justify your request, but it may help to briefly state why you feel a supervisor is necessary. If your request is denied, note the officer's name, badge number, and the time of the request. This information can be useful if you choose to file a formal complaint later.

Can an officer stop you outside of their jurisdiction?

Jurisdiction refers to the geographical area or legal boundaries within which a police officer has the authority to enforce laws, conduct stops, make arrests, and carry out other duties. Jurisdictional limits are essential because they help to define the scope of an officer's authority.

For example, city police generally have authority only within city limits, while county sheriffs operate within county boundaries. State troopers, meanwhile, can often enforce laws statewide. However, there are several circumstances where an officer may be allowed to act outside of their official jurisdiction.

In some states, like Arizona, officers are granted statewide authority, meaning that any sworn police officer can make a stop or an arrest anywhere in their state. Additionally, the doctrine of "fresh pursuit," also known as "hot pursuit," allows officers to cross jurisdictional lines if they are actively pursuing a suspect who is fleeing. This exception is recognized in most states and is designed to prevent suspects from escaping simply by crossing into a different jurisdiction.

In some areas, mutual aid agreements exist between neighboring jurisdictions, allowing officers to assist one another in enforcement activities. For example, neighboring cities might have agreements allowing their officers to cross jurisdictional lines when providing assistance during emergencies or when pursuing a suspect. Officers may also act outside their jurisdiction during emergency situations that require immediate attention, such as to prevent serious harm or protect public safety.

These situations often involve exigent circumstances,

meaning there is an immediate need for action to prevent harm or prevent the destruction of evidence. It is also worth noting that, in certain situations, officers who are outside their jurisdiction can make a citizen's arrest. Under the law, any citizen has the authority to make an arrest if they witness a felony being committed. If an officer is off-duty or out of their jurisdiction but sees a felony taking place, they can make an arrest just as any private citizen could.

Contesting whether an officer is within their jurisdiction to stop or arrest you is a matter that should be reserved for the courtroom. If you find yourself questioning the jurisdictional authority of an officer during your own encounter, it is best to comply with the stop and the commands of the officer and challenge his authority later in court. There are so many factors that could influence the jurisdictional authority of a police officer that would be impossible to know during the encounter, and compliance is the best way to ensure your safety and the integrity of your court case.

Interacting with law enforcement officers in public spaces can be unexpected and stressful, but preparedness and awareness are the keys to success when navigating these types of police encounters. Remember that while the letter of the law provides a framework, your demeanor and approach are what put that framework into action. A polite request for a supervisor or a calm invocation of your right to remain silent can sometimes do more to protect your rights than knowing the most detailed legal precedent. Knowing the boundaries of what law enforcement can and cannot do is not just an abstract exercise in understanding the law, but a practical toolkit that can profoundly shape the way you approach these encounters.

Chapter Eight
Encountering Police on the Road

In 2020, The Stanford Open Policing Project, which is sponsored by Stanford University, released a study finding that police officers conduct more that 50,000 traffic stops on an average day. That's over 20 million traffic stops per year. The odds that you will be involved in a traffic stop at some point in your life are a near statistical inevitability.

Traffic stops are fundamentally different from any other interaction with law enforcement because vehicles introduce significantly more safety risks for everyone involved. Not only do traffic stops typically occur along dangerous roadways and intersections, but officers are particularly vulnerable to the occupants of the vehicles they approach. This has led courts to grant officers a higher degree of control over these types of interactions, but your constitutional rights must still be respected regardless of the situation. Not to mention the fact that many officers are trained to view traffic stops as inherently dangerous and difficult to manage.

Understanding and asserting your rights during traffic stops can be a difficult and nuanced task, but grasping a few fundamental legal concepts, along with some practical recommendations, can dramatically improve the likelihood of successfully navigating these types of encounters.

How to Avoid a Traffic Stop

The first step to successfully navigating a traffic stop is to avoid one altogether. Although there is no guaranteed way to completely avoid a traffic stop, you can significantly reduce your chances by practicing good driving habits, keeping your vehicle in excellent condition, and being mindful of your actions on the road.

One of the most common reasons for being pulled over is vehicle-related issues. Proper vehicle maintenance not only keeps you safe but also helps avoid drawing unnecessary attention from law enforcement. Officers are more likely to pull you over if your vehicle is visibly non-compliant with traffic laws or appears unsafe.

Make sure your headlights, taillights, brake lights, and turn signals are functioning properly. A broken taillight or a missing headlight is a simple issue that can lead to a traffic stop. Ensure your license plate is visible and properly secured. Some drivers get pulled over simply because their license plate is obscured by dirt, snow, or a cover that makes it hard to read.

Check that your registration tags are up-to-date and properly displayed. Expired registration tags can easily prompt an officer to pull you over, even if you are otherwise driving responsibly. The laws regarding vehicle maintenance and equipment violations vary from state to state, as well as the degree to which officers are authorized to enforce those laws. Making sure that your vehicle is compliant to state regulations is one of the most practical ways to avoid being stopped by the police.

While this may seem obvious, your driving behavior is another major factor in whether or not you will be stopped by law enforcement. Speeding is one of the most common reasons for traffic stops, and can be one of the more difficult police encounters to navigate without unintentionally incriminating yourself. Failing to use your turn signals is another simple but frequent reason for traffic stops. Distracted driving is yet another growing concern and a major reason for traffic stops.

If an officer sees you texting, holding your phone, or otherwise distracted, you could be stopped, and familiarizing yourself with your state's laws on cell phone usage while driving is advisable. Practicing safe driving habits and obeying the rules of the road may seem like trivial advice, yet minor traffic violations continue to be a major catalyst for police interactions in general.

Even if you follow every rule perfectly, it is still possible to be pulled over by law enforcement. Officers have broad discretion, and sometimes factors beyond your control, like matching the description of a suspect vehicle, can lead to a stop. However, by taking proactive steps to reduce the reasons an officer might pull you over, you can minimize the likelihood of such encounters and ensure that if you are pulled over, it's not because of a preventable issue.

Although no method is foolproof, reducing visible vehicle issues and avoiding common driving errors can significantly minimize your risk of being pulled over. The best strategy is to stay aware, stay calm, and stay informed so that if you are pulled over, it happens under the best possible circumstances, where you have taken every precaution to ensure compliance with the law.

What to Do When Being Pulled Over

The first thing you should do when you realize a police officer wants to pull you over is to stay calm and prepare to pull over safely. Panicking or making sudden movements can lead to dangerous driving and misunderstood intent, so it's important to remain composed.

If an officer is behind you with lights flashing, use your turn signal to indicate that you are acknowledging them and are preparing to pull over. This gesture tells the officer that you're aware of their presence and that you intend to comply. Find a safe place to pull over. Ideally, you want to choose a spot where you can safely stop without obstructing traffic.

If you're on a highway, use the shoulder; in urban areas, try to pull over in a parking lot or well-lit area to ensure visibility for both you and the officer. Don't brake suddenly. Gradually reduce your speed, allowing the officer time to anticipate your movements. Abrupt braking could create a dangerous situation, especially if there is heavy traffic.

Once you have stopped, put your vehicle in park and turn off the engine. Turning off the engine signals to the officer that you do not intend to flee, and it shows compliance. In some cases, like at night or in areas with poor visibility, turning on your hazard lights can help ensure that passing drivers are aware of your vehicle and the traffic stop.

If the stop takes place at night, turning on your interior lighting will enhance the officer's sense of safety and help the interaction start off on a good note. If you have dark tinted windows then you might also consider rolling all of your windows down so that the officer can clearly see inside your vehicle and quickly ascertain no threats are present.

Keeping your hands in plan view at all times will also help the officer feel more safe, and having the proper documentation, such as your license, insurance, and vehicle registration, before the officer approaches your vehicle will help speed things along. Be sure to keep your documentation in an area that is easily accessible, as rummaging through your vehicle to find your insurance or registration as the officer approaches may create more suspicion than convenience. The less time you have to spend in a traffic stop, the better.

Once an officer approaches your vehicle the way you interact with them can significantly influence how the stop proceeds. It is important to remain respectful and cooperative, while also being mindful of your rights. When the officer approaches your window, greet them politely. A simple "Good evening, officer" can help set a positive tone for the interaction.

As we discussed in previous chapters, not everything you say to a police officer is incriminating, and it can be a good idea to politely respond to innocent questions like "How are you doing?" in an effort to establish rapport with the officer. However, it is equally important to remember that you are not required to answer questions such as "Do you know why I pulled you over?" or "Do you know how fast you were going?" These questions are often used to gather evidence of guilt.

In situations like this, you might consider responding with "I don't believe I committed a crime. Can you tell me why I was stopped?" or "Respectfully officer, I know how fast I was going, but I would prefer not to comment further without my attorney present." If the officer asks probing questions unrelated to the reason for the stop, such as whether you have anything illegal in the car, you can politely decline to answer. Simply say, "Officer, I choose not to answer any questions without legal representation." Remaining polite and being prepared are the keys to preventing the situation from escalating.

If you are the driver of the vehicle you are required to present your ID to the officer who stopped you. In some states you are only required to show your ID, but in others, you may be required to give it to the officers. Regardless of your state's law, allowing an officer to take possession of your ID does nothing to incriminate you in any way, and starting a meaningless debate about whether or not the officer has the authority to take your ID, or merely see it, only serves to escalate and prolong the interaction. If you are involved in a traffic stop it is best to hand over your license, registration, and insurance at the officer's request to avoid unnecessary escalation.

If you are a passenger in a vehicle the requirement to present ID becomes much more nuanced. As discussed in previous chapters, passengers, like drivers, have constitutional rights, and an important part of these rights includes freedom from unreasonable searches and seizures. However, passengers do not enjoy absolute immunity from having to identify themselves during a traffic stop.

Unlike drivers, passengers are not always legally required to identify themselves simply because they are present in a vehicle that has been pulled over, however, if an officer suspects the passenger of a crime outside of the initial traffic stop they may initiate an investigative detention of them. For example, if an officer stops a vehicle in a state where marijuana is illegal and detects the odor of marijuana, they would likely be within their authority to identify any passengers inside the vehicle, as they will be investigated for possession of marijuana, not the initial traffic infraction.

Quick Tip: There are no laws that require police officers to tell you why they have pulled you over and they may withhold this information until you comply with their requests. However, departments typically have policies that require officers to inform citizens of why they are being stopped. If an officer refuses to tell you why you have been pulled over, document it and file a complaint with the department, and peacefully comply with the rest of the stop.

How you handle the conclusion of a traffic stop is just as important as how it began. Whether you are given a warning, a citation, or let go without further action, it's important to end the interaction respectfully and safely. If it is unclear whether the traffic stop is over, you can politely ask, "Officer, am I free to go?" This is especially helpful if the conversation seems to be dragging on without a clear resolution.

Knowing when the stop is officially over prevents confusion about whether you can leave. Always wait for the officer to return to their vehicle or give you clear instruction to leave. Avoid starting your engine or moving your vehicle before the officer has stepped away, as this can be seen as an attempt to flee.

Vehicle Searches

During a traffic stop, one of the most concerning questions for drivers is whether the police can search their vehicle and, if so, under what circumstances. As discussed in the previous chapter, the answer is not always straightforward, as it depends on a combination of your rights under the Fourth Amendment and exceptions to those rights.

The Fourth Amendment protects citizens from unreasonable searches and seizures, and this extends to vehicle searches. However, because vehicles are inherently mobile and often exposed to public view, courts have provided law enforcement with more considerable leeway in searching vehicles compared to homes.

Just like any other search, a warrant is typically required to search a vehicle, however, the same exceptions that apply to other searches, such as exigent circumstances, searches incident to arrest, and consent searches, also apply. For example, if an officer witnesses an individual destroying contraband inside their car, the officer would be within their authority to search the car under the exigent circumstances exception.

Similarly, if you are arrested during a traffic stop you can be searched without a warrant as a search incident to arrest exception. If your car is towed, the officers can also conduct an inventory search, where they will document, and sometimes confiscate, all of the personal items in your car for you to retrieve later. If the officers happen to discover illegal contraband or weapons during this search, it could result in additional charges.

Not only do drivers and passengers have to contend with traditional exceptions to the Fourth Amendment's protections against unreasonable search and seizure, but the Supreme Court also carved out a special exception to the warrant requirement known as the "Automobile Exception." This exception allows law enforcement to search a vehicle without a warrant if they have probable cause to believe that the vehicle contains evidence of a crime. Going back to the example from earlier, if an officer detects the odor of marijuana this would generally grant them probable cause to search the vehicle under the automobile exception.

Understanding what parts of your vehicle can be searched during a traffic stop depends on the specific legal justification the officer has for the search. If an officer has probable cause, or you give them consent to search, they are generally authorized to search every part of your vehicle and all of the containers, such as purses or duffle bags, that are inside of it. Even locked containers, like safes or briefcases, can be opened if the police have probable cause to believe they may contain evidence related to a crime.

The right to be free from unreasonable searches is a fundamental aspect of the Fourth Amendment, but that right is not absolute, particularly when it comes to vehicles. If you are pulled over and the officer asks to search your vehicle, always remember that you have the right to refuse consent even if the officer has a legal basis to proceed without it. If an officer demands to search your vehicle then it is best to comply, as there may be factors at play that justify their search that you are not aware of. If you believe the search was conducted unlawfully then you can challenge the legality of the search in the courtroom.

Quick Tip: Informing the officer that you do not consent to any searches, regardless of the perceived legality of the search, can potentially serve you well if the search is later found to be unlawful.

What is a citation?

During a traffic stop, you may be issued a citation, often referred to as a "ticket." A citation is essentially a formal notice given to a driver by a law enforcement officer, informing them that they have violated a traffic law. It serves as an alternative to arrest for minor offenses, allowing drivers to continue on their way without being taken into custody.

The citation will generally include information about the alleged offense, the date and time, the location, and instructions for either paying the fine or contesting the citation in court.

The purpose of issuing a citation is to avoid arresting individuals for minor offenses, such as speeding or running a stop sign. A citation allows drivers to either pay the fine or schedule a court date to contest the charges without the need for detention. A citation is also a form of formal notice that you are being charged with a specific traffic violation. It is not a determination of guilt but rather an official statement that an officer believes you have committed an infraction. A citation is meant to avoid arrest and provide drivers with an opportunity to resolve the matter without being detained, but the officer has discretion to arrest if circumstances warrant it.

When issued a citation, you may be asked to sign it. Signing a citation has absolutely no bearing on whether or not you will be found guilty for the crime you are being charged with, and there is no legitimate reason to refuse to sign a citation. The law regarding whether or not you are required to sign a citation varies significantly from state to state, but even in states where you are not legally obligated to sign a citation, there is no reason to refuse to sign.

Not only does refusing to sign a citation create an unnecessarily hostile relationship with the officer, but it will likely be difficult to explain to a judge or jury why you refused to do so. In states where you are legally obligated to sign the citations you've been issued, a refusal to sign will likely result in your arrest.

Signing the ticket means you are committing to either pay the fine associated with the citation or appear in court to contest the charge. The officer will typically provide instructions on how to do either, including deadlines and methods of payment. If you sign the citation but fail to follow through, either by not paying the fine or by failing to appear in court, a warrant may be issued for your arrest. In some states, failing to address a citation can lead to additional fines or even suspension of your driver's license.

Can the police order you out of your vehicle?

During a traffic stop, one of the more unsettling aspects for drivers and passengers can be an officer's request, or demand, that they step out of the vehicle. Police officers have broad discretion when it comes to ordering drivers and passengers out of a vehicle during a traffic stop. These requests are rooted in concerns about officer safety, as traffic stops are often unpredictable and can pose potential risks.

Two key Supreme Court cases, Pennsylvania v. Mimms and Maryland v. Wilson, have established that officers can lawfully order both drivers and passengers out of a vehicle without needing additional justification beyond the traffic stop itself. Anytime an officer orders you or any of your passengers to remain inside or get out of the vehicle during a lawful traffic stop, you must obey their command. Contrary to popular belief, officers do not need a specific reason to order a driver or passenger to get out of the vehicle, and refusing to obey this command will almost certainly result in your arrest.

Is there a time limit to traffic stops?

The duration of a traffic stop is a critical factor in determining its legality. Under the Fourth Amendment to the Constitution, citizens are protected from unreasonable seizures, and this protection extends to traffic stops. The Supreme Court has established that officers must conduct traffic stops in a diligent and efficient manner and must not extend the duration of the stop beyond what is reasonably necessary to achieve the original purpose of the stop unless additional reasonable suspicion arises.

As discussed in previous chapters, the duration of a stop can vary depending on the circumstances surrounding the stop, however, the duration of a stop must be tied to the purpose for which you were initially stopped. This means that the officer should only detain you for as long as it takes to complete tasks such as checking your driver's license, vehicle registration, issuing a citation, or verifying insurance. Once these tasks are completed, you should be allowed to go unless new reasonable suspicion or probable cause arises.

The determination of what constitutes a "reasonable" duration for a traffic stop is based on the specific circumstances of each encounter. Courts will evaluate the nature of the stop, the officer's conduct, and whether the officer was acting diligently in fulfilling the purpose of the stop. Checking for outstanding warrants, verifying vehicle registration, and contacting dispatch to confirm insurance information are all tasks that may add time to a stop but are generally considered reasonable.

A minor traffic violation, such as speeding or running a stop sign, typically requires a short duration for the officer to issue a warning or citation. If the stop takes significantly longer than expected for such minor violations, it may be deemed unreasonable. If new evidence or reasonable suspicion emerges during the stop, for example, if the officer notices drug paraphernalia in plain view or smells alcohol, the officer may extend the stop to investigate further. This extension is permissible as long as it is directly related to the new evidence and conducted within a reasonable timeframe.

Officers may ask unrelated questions during a traffic stop, such as inquiries about your travel plans or whether you have anything illegal in the car, as long as these questions do not measurably extend the duration of the stop. The key is whether the officer's conduct deviates from the original purpose of the stop and whether it unnecessarily prolongs your detention.

If you find yourself in a traffic stop where the officer appears to be delaying the stop without clear justification, you can politely ask, "Officer, am I free to go?" This question prompts the officer to clarify whether they have completed the tasks necessary for the stop or if they have additional reasons for detaining you. Although the officer is not required to be truthful to you, their on-the-fly answers may be difficult to explain to a judge or jury.

When can the police use a canine?

The use of specially trained dogs that can detect drugs, explosives, or other contraband can significantly impact the rights of drivers and passengers during a traffic stop. In many traffic stops, officers may call for a canine unit to assist in determining whether there are drugs or other contraband inside a vehicle. Anytime the police use a dog to search the interior of a vehicle they need probable cause or a warrant, however, officers may use a canine to sniff the exterior of a vehicle at any time during a lawful traffic stop.

According to the 2005 Supreme Court case of Illinois v. Caballes, using a dog to sniff the exterior of a vehicle is not considered a search under the Fourth Amendment, however, it cannot prolong the stop beyond the time necessary to handle the original reason for the stop. The duration of a traffic stop should be limited to the time it takes to address the reason for the stop, such as issuing a citation or warning, checking the driver's license, and verifying registration and insurance.

If calling a canine unit extends the stop without any additional evidence or reasonable suspicion, the stop could become unlawful. If an officer wishes to detain you longer than is necessary to handle the original reason for the stop in order to wait for a canine unit, they need reasonable suspicion that you are engaged in illegal activity beyond a minor traffic infraction.

For example, if an officer notices that you appear extremely nervous, are giving inconsistent answers, or if there is the odor of drugs coming from the car, these factors might provide reasonable suspicion to justify extending the stop until a canine unit arrives.

When a traffic stop has been completed and the officer no longer has a reason to detain you, extending the stop just to wait for a canine unit without reasonable suspicion is generally considered an unreasonable delay. As we discussed in the previous section, the duration of a traffic stop must be reasonable based on the circumstances, and officers cannot use a canine unit to unreasonably delay your detention, as doing so would constitute an unlawful seizure under the Fourth Amendment. However, officers are granted a considerable amount of time to conduct a traffic stop and will likely have ample time to summon a canine unit to the scene while they're working on the administrative aspects of the stop.

If an officer informs you that a canine unit is coming to the scene, it is important to remain calm and comply with any lawful orders, but also document when the canine arrives, as this could be valuable information in a courtroom. If you feel that the wait for the canine unit is excessive, you can politely ask the officer, "Am I free to go?" This question is important because it prompts the officer to clarify whether they still have a legitimate reason to detain you. If the officer says you are not free to go, you may ask, "Officer, may I ask why I am being detained?" If a canine unit arrives and alerts to the presence of contraband, leading to a search of your vehicle, but you believe that the stop was unlawfully prolonged, you may have grounds to challenge the search in court. The evidence gathered may be deemed inadmissible if the court determines that the stop was extended without reasonable suspicion.

DUI Checkpoints

DUI checkpoints, also known as sobriety checkpoints, are temporary roadblocks set up by law enforcement to identify and deter drivers under the influence of alcohol or drugs.

Unlike standard traffic stops, DUI checkpoints involve stopping drivers without any reasonable suspicion of wrongdoing. The constitutionality of these checkpoints has been a topic of debate, and the Supreme Court has provided guidance on when and how such checkpoints can be conducted. In the 1990 case of Michigan Department of State Police v. Sitz the Court ruled that DUI checkpoints are constitutional as long as they are conducted in a reasonable manner. The Court found that the need to prevent drunk driving and promote public safety outweighs the minimal intrusion on individual rights.

While the Supreme Court has upheld the constitutionality of DUI checkpoints, their legality varies from state to state. Some states have additional privacy protections that prohibit DUI checkpoints altogether. Most states allow DUI checkpoints as long as they are conducted according to specific guidelines to minimize arbitrary enforcement. Law enforcement agencies must announce the location and timing of checkpoints in advance to provide transparency to the public. However, states such as Texas and Oregon do not allow DUI checkpoints, considering them to be unconstitutional under their state constitutions. In these states, law enforcement must rely on reasonable suspicion or probable cause to conduct DUI stops.

The goal of a checkpoint is to identify drivers who may be under the influence, but the process also includes ensuring compliance with other vehicle regulations. Officers are not required to ignore equipment violations, or any other crime, simply because their original intent was to determine your sobriety. If your tag is expired or your headlight is out, officers can issue a citation for those violations during a DUI checkpoint.

While at a DUI checkpoint an officer may ask for your

driver's license, registration, and proof of insurance. They may also observe your demeanor and look for signs of impairment, such as slurred speech, bloodshot eyes, or alcohol odor. If the officer reasonably suspects that you may be under the influence based on their initial observation, they may request that you pull aside for further screening, which could potentially include a field sobriety test or a breathalyzer test.

Whether or not you are required to submit to sobriety tests or chemical testing varies dramatically from state to state, and you might consider taking time to understand your state's laws regarding your legal obligations during a DUI stop. In most states, refusing a breathalyzer test carries implied consent consequences, such as automatic license suspension. This is because by driving, you have implicitly agreed to chemical testing if lawfully arrested for suspicion of driving under the influence.

Quick Tip: In most jurisdictions, you are legally allowed to turn around to avoid a DUI checkpoint, as long as you do so lawfully without violating any traffic laws or driving in an otherwise erratic manner. However, if an officer sees you making an abrupt or illegal U-turn to avoid the checkpoint, this could create reasonable suspicion for the officer to stop you. It's important to follow traffic laws and avoid any erratic behavior if you decide to turn away from a checkpoint.

Always remember that you have the right to remain silent beyond providing necessary documents. If an officer asks where you are coming from or whether you have been drinking, you can respond with, "Officer, I have not consumed any illegal or mind altering substances today. Respectfully, I prefer not to answer any questions without an attorney present."

Traffic stops are one of the most complex types of police interactions that a citizen can experience, and ironically, they are also the most common. Remember that while officers have the authority to stop you for a legitimate reason, they must conduct their duties within the bounds of the law, including keeping stops as brief as possible. Stay calm, remain polite, comply with lawful orders, and assert your rights when necessary. By knowing what officers are legally allowed to do and what your responsibilities are, you can protect yourself, minimize unnecessary conflict, and ensure that your rights are respected throughout the encounter.

Chapter Nine
Encountering Police at Home

Of all the places you might encounter the police, your home offers you the most protection in terms of constitutional rights. The Supreme Court has consistently recognized that a person's home is a sacred place where they should enjoy the highest degree of privacy and constitutional protection.

What is unique about private property is that different parts of your property may be subject to different legal standards depending on the circumstances of the interaction. Whether police officers are knocking on your front door or standing out in your cow pasture can make a significant difference in the legality of their conduct, and not every situation involving private property is resolved simply by ordering the police to leave. Although your constitutional protections are the strongest inside your home, not all areas of your property enjoy the same level of protection, and there are several factors to consider whenever you're dealing with the police on your own property. Nonetheless, you are protected from police misconduct on your own property, but knowing how to navigate this type of encounter can be trickier than it initially appears.

Do the police need a warrant to enter your property?

Generally, the police do need a warrant to enter your home or the area immediately surrounding it, but there are important distinctions between different parts of your property, and certain exceptions to the warrant requirement may apply depending on the circumstances.

A search of the home is just like any other search, it requires the officers to have a warrant or an exception to the warrant requirement, just as they would if they were searching your vehicle. The same exceptions to the warrant requirement that apply to other searches also apply to searches of the home. So for instance, if an officer witnesses someone being assaulted inside your home through an open window, they would be within their authority to enter your home without a warrant to stop the assault under the exigent circumstances doctrine we discussed throughout this book.

Different parts of your property enjoy different degrees of constitutional protection. The area immediately surrounding your home, which is known as the "curtilage," carries a similar expectation of privacy as the home itself. This includes structures like porches, fenced yards, garages, and patios. Curtilage is protected by the Fourth Amendment, and officers generally need a warrant to enter these areas.

On the other hand, large plots of land, fields, and forests on your property do not enjoy the same protections under the Fourth Amendment. Under the "Open Fields Doctrine," areas of land that are not intimately tied to the home, such as large pastures, forests, deserts, or farmlands, are not subject to Fourth

Amendment protections because no reasonable expectation of privacy exists there.

This means that police officers can enter and observe open areas of private property without a warrant or probable cause. Even if you have a fence and 'No Trespassing' signs posted all over your property, police officers are within their authority to enter any area that is considered an 'open field' by the courts.

As a practical example, imagine that officers arrive at your home following up on a tip about possible criminal activity. They see a gate to your fenced backyard but decide to enter without knocking on the front door or obtaining a warrant. This entry could be challenged as unconstitutional because your fenced backyard is considered part of the curtilage of your home, and the officers did not have a warrant, consent, or exigent circumstances that justified their entry.

Now suppose you own a large piece of property that includes a house, a fenced backyard, and several acres of farmland. Police officers receive a tip that there may be illegal drug activity occurring on the farmland. They enter the property through a gate marked with "No Trespassing" signs and cross the farmland without a warrant. Under the Open Fields Doctrine, officers do not need a warrant to enter that area, and the "No Trespassing" signs do not create a reasonable expectation of privacy.

It should also be noted that police officers are generally permitted to approach your home and knock on your front door. As far as the courts are concerned, the whole purpose of a front door is so that people can come and knock on it to see if you're home. There is an implied invitation for visitors to walk up to your front door and knock on it. Police officers are permitted to knock on your front door just as any other citizen would be, however, this does not permit officers to enter areas that are clearly marked as private or are enclosed.

Quick Tip: Even with a valid warrant, officers are usually required to knock and announce their presence before entering.

Not only can the police enter your home if they have a search warrant, but they can also enter your home if they have an arrest warrant for you or someone who lives with you. When officers enter a home to make an arrest, their authority is generally limited to finding the person named in the arrest warrant. They may look for the individual in areas where the person could reasonably be found, but this does not mean they can search unrelated areas of the home or personal belongings unless they have a separate search warrant. Officers may also seize evidence or contraband if it is in plain view.

Quick Tip: If police have an arrest warrant for a suspect at their own home, they can enter that residence if they have reason to believe the suspect is present. However, to enter a third party's home to execute an arrest warrant, they need both the arrest warrant for the suspect and a separate search warrant for the third party's premises

Anytime the police enter your home it would be wise to clearly state that you do not consent to any searches or seizures, regardless of whether or not the officers have a warrant. This ensures that nothing you did or said could be construed as consent to search further or otherwise extend the limitations of the warrant. If the police inform you that they have a warrant to search your property or arrest a person inside your home, it is always in your best interest to comply with the officers and challenge the legality of their conduct later in court.

Do you have Fourth Amendment rights as a tenant?

As a tenant, you enjoy the same Fourth Amendment rights in your home as homeowners do, and your right to privacy extends to your rented apartment or house. Whether you rent a single-family house, an apartment, or a room in a larger dwelling, you are entitled to the same privacy expectations as a homeowner. The police cannot enter your rented space without your permission or the special circumstances mentioned in the previous section.

A landlord does not have the authority to allow the police to enter your private living space without your permission. Even though the landlord owns the property, they cannot give law enforcement consent to search or enter your unit unless there is an emergency, such as a fire, gas leak, or other immediate safety threat.

Quick Tip: If a landlord enters your unit for routine maintenance or repairs, they cannot invite law enforcement to accompany them or allow officers to search your belongings. Such an entry is strictly limited to the purpose of maintaining the property and does not override your Fourth Amendment protections.

In shared living situations, such as renting a room in a house where other tenants occupy separate rooms, each tenant retains a reasonable expectation of privacy in their individual space. This means that police officers would need a warrant to search your private room, even if they receive consent from another tenant to enter the common areas of the home. While a roommate can give consent for police to enter shared or common areas of the home, such as the kitchen, living room, or shared bathroom, they cannot consent to the search of your private room or any locked containers belonging exclusively to you. If the police wish to search your personal areas, they will need either your consent, a warrant, or a warrant exception.

In apartment buildings, common areas such as hallways, lobbies, laundry rooms, and parking garages are not typically considered private spaces. Police officers may enter and observe these areas without a warrant because tenants generally do not have a reasonable expectation of privacy in common spaces that are accessible to other residents or the general public. It is important to note that the notion of privacy in common areas of apartment buildings and other shared living spaces is still a developing topic among higher courts, and the legal precedents surrounding this topic may vary depending on which jurisdiction you are in.

Another point to consider regarding rented property is the terms and obligations of your lease. There may be situations where you are obligated to waive certain privacy rights as a condition of renting the space. This can include routine inspections of the space, or even an agreement to submit to the presence of officers on the property. For example, if you rent a building for your business, the property owner may have an existing agreement with the local police that allows them to park on the property. This might be a stipulation that the owner of the property could incorporate into the lease agreement.

A rented space is treated the same as an owned home as far as the courts are concerned, and you should not hesitate to assert the same rights in an apartment or rented space as you would on property that you privately own. Being a tenant does not diminish your right to privacy or any of your other constitutional protections, however, it is important to pay attention to the details of your lease and ensure that you conduct any private activities inside your rented space, not in the common areas of the property.

Welfare Checks

A "welfare check," also known as a "wellness check," is a visit conducted by law enforcement to check on the well-being of an individual. Welfare checks are usually prompted by someone expressing concern for a person's safety or health, such as family members, neighbors, or friends. A welfare check is intended to ensure the safety and well-being of an individual who may be in danger or experiencing a medical emergency, and is often requested when someone is unresponsive to calls or texts, has not been seen for an unusually long period, or if there are signs of distress. Welfare checks can be initiated by family members, neighbors, friends, or even by employers if someone fails to show up for work. Sometimes, social services may also request a welfare check on a vulnerable individual, such as an elderly person or someone with mental health challenges, who has not been heard from recently.

Police officers are not allowed to enter a home during a welfare check without consent or a warrant, however, if officers come across evidence of criminal activity in the course of a welfare check, such as seeing illegal substances in plain view or smelling narcotics, this may provide them with probable cause to take further action. If officers develop probable cause based on what they see or smell, they may be justified in entering the home under exigent circumstances to prevent the destruction of evidence, render emergency aid, or to address an immediate threat.

If you become the subject of an unwanted welfare check, dispelling the safety concerns of the officer should be your highest priority. Clearly inform the officer that you are not in need of any emergency services and work to terminate the encounter as quickly as possible without acting suspicious. Welfare checks are often used by the police as gateways to deeper investigations, and spending as little time as necessary to reassure the officer that you are fine will hopefully rob the officer of any opportunity to develop reasonable suspicion or probable cause.

Due to the fact that officers responding to welfare checks are typically on alert for signs of mental distress or impairment, it can be difficult to convince an officer that you are not in need of help. Calmly stating something like "Officer, I am not a threat to myself or anyone else and I do not require emergency services. I am respectfully asking you to leave now," can help to dispel the officer's safety concerns while also asserting your rights peacefully. Remember that remaining calm and collected is especially important during welfare checks, as you may be dealing with officers who are on alert, and asserting your rights diligently is the key to navigating these types of encounters successfully.

What to Do if the Police Knock on Your Door

As mentioned before, police officers are within their authority to knock on your front door if it is not blocked by a clearly marked barrier, but you are not required to answer your door unless the officers have a warrant.

When the police knock on your door, it can be an intimidating experience, but here are a few practical considerations that might help you successfully navigate this type of encounter:

1. Observe Before You Answer: Remember that you do not have to answer your door if the police do not have a warrant. However, if you are considering answering the door, try to observe who is at the door by looking through a peephole, window, or security camera if available. This may give you clues about their intentions.

2. Document Their Presence: It may be useful to document the situation before answering. This could include taking a picture of the officers through a window, noting the time and date, or turning on a security camera. Documentation can be valuable later if you need to reference what happened.

3. Limit the Interaction Through the Door: Whenever possible, limit your interaction to speaking through the closed door. This ensures that your privacy is maintained, and it reduces the likelihood that the officers will interpret any of your actions as suspicious. If you need to open the door, consider using a chain lock or a door latch that allows the door to open slightly but still provides a physical barrier. This allows you to speak to the officers while keeping a level of security in place.

4. Determine Their Intentions: You have the right to know why the police are knocking on your door. You can ask them through the door, "What is the purpose of your visit?" They may be there for a welfare check, investigation, to serve a warrant, or some other legitimate reason you are not aware of.

5. Ask for Identification: It is always appropriate to ask officers to identify themselves, including showing a badge or other credentials. This helps confirm that they are legitimate law enforcement officers and gives you a record of who was present at your door.

6. Do Not Answer Unnecessary Questions: If officers are asking you questions as part of an investigation, you have the right not to answer. You can say, "I do not wish to answer any questions without my attorney present." This helps protect your rights and prevents you from inadvertently providing information that could be used against you. Refusing entry may feel intimidating, but it is important to remember that this is a protected right. The police cannot legally enter your home without a warrant or emergency, even if they attempt to persuade or pressure you.

7. Explicitly Refuse Entry Without a Warrant: If officers do not have a warrant, you are legally within your rights to refuse entry. You can say something like, "I do not consent to any search of my home, and I do not wish to answer any questions without my attorney present."

8. Do Not Give Implied Consent: Be careful not to give officers implied consent to enter. For example, stepping aside or saying something like "Sure, come in" can be interpreted as allowing them to enter freely. If you do not want the officers to enter, be clear and direct in refusing consent.

9. Record the Interaction: Your right to record enjoys the most protections on private property and there is no legitimate reason why you shouldn't record as much as possible when interacting with the police on your own property. It would also be a good idea to write down key details, such as the names and badge numbers of the officers, the time and date of the encounter, and the reason they provided for their visit. This information can be useful if you need to follow up with the police department or take legal action.

10. Comply, but Assert Your Rights: If officers have a search warrant, you must comply and allow them to enter, but you can still protect your rights by observing and documenting their actions. Remember that officers are within their authority to detain you while they execute a search. Politely state that you do not consent to any additional searches beyond what is authorized by the warrant. If the officers do not detain you, it is a good idea to observe the search as closely as possible to ensure that they do not exceed the scope of the warrant. Take notes or record the interaction if possible to document what the officers are doing. Remember that challenging the legality of a search warrant should take place within a courtroom, not at your house.

Your home is your sanctuary, and the rights guaranteed by the Constitution reflect this deeply rooted societal value. Protecting your home from government intrusion is about more than just legal protocols; it's about understanding that, while law enforcement has a role to play, your autonomy and dignity as an individual are equally as important. Knowing your rights is not about antagonism; it's about preserving the sanctity of your space, recognizing the boundaries that both you and law enforcement must respect, and fostering more positive and respectful interactions with the police. Awareness, clarity, and self-control are your greatest tools in ensuring your home remains the haven it is meant to be, even when the unexpected knock comes at your door.

Chapter Ten
What to Do After an Encounter

Experiencing a police encounter can be a jarring and emotionally charged event, leaving you feeling unsettled, confused, or even traumatized. Many citizens struggle to emotionally process negative police interactions, and aren't sure where to even begin with seeking justice. What you choose to do after an encounter with the police can be just as vital as the choices you make during an interaction, and finding and utilizing the proper avenues for justice is no small task.

This is especially true for citizens who are encountering the police or experiencing police misconduct for the first time. The whirlwind of emotions following a negative police interaction often overwhelms unprepared individuals and leaves them in a cloud of confusion. Arming yourself with the knowledge of what to do after an encounter can better prepare you for the actual encounters themselves and put you one step ahead of a bad officer. There are a number of things to do after a police encounter, particularly if it involves an allegation of misconduct. Simply showing up for your court date will not suffice in a battle against bad police behavior, and familiarizing yourself with what to do after a negative interaction is absolutley essential.

Immediate Action Post-Encounter

Whether the interaction was brief and uneventful or tense and confrontational, the moments immediately following are crucial. How you choose to act in this period can significantly influence any future legal proceedings, complaints, or resolutions related to the encounter. It's essential to approach this time with a clear mind and a purposeful plan to protect your rights and interests.

As soon as the encounter concludes, it's important to find a quiet space where you can gather your thoughts. The adrenaline and stress hormones coursing through your body may cloud your judgment, so taking a moment to breathe deeply and calm yourself is beneficial. This pause allows you to transition from a reactive state to a more reflective one, enabling you to think more clearly about the steps you need to take.

One of the most immediate and important actions is to document everything about the encounter while the details are still fresh in your mind. Human memory is notoriously unreliable, especially under stress, and key details can fade quickly. Find a notebook, use a notes app on your phone, or even record a voice memo to capture your recollections. Begin by noting the date, time, and location of the incident. Describe the environment: Was it daytime or nighttime? What was the weather like? Were there any notable landmarks or nearby businesses?

Next, focus on the specifics of the interaction. Write down the names and badge numbers of the officers involved if you were able to obtain them. If not, provide detailed physical descriptions, including approximate age, height, build, ethnicity, and any distinguishing features such as tattoos or unique uniforms. Note the number of officers present and whether they were in uniform or plainclothes. Describe any police vehicles, including license plate numbers if possible.

Recount the sequence of events as accurately as you can remember. Detail what the officers said to you and how you responded. Use direct quotes where possible, especially for significant statements or commands. Include any questions they asked and your replies. Be honest and objective in your account; avoid embellishments or assumptions about the officers' intentions. Stick to the facts as you perceive them.

If there were witnesses to the encounter, their observations could be invaluable. Look around to see if anyone was present during the incident. This could include pedestrians, shop owners, passengers in your vehicle, or even bystanders recording with their phones. Approach them politely, explain that you may need their account of what happened, and ask for their contact information. Get their names, phone numbers, and email addresses. If they are willing, have them provide a brief statement of what they saw and heard. Witness testimony can lend credibility to your version of events and may be critical in any legal proceedings.

Preserving any physical evidence related to the encounter is another essential step. If you sustained any injuries, no matter how minor, photograph them from multiple angles. Use a camera with a timestamp function if possible. Continue to document the healing process over the following days, as some injuries may become more apparent with time. If your property was damaged—for example, if your car was searched and items were broken or misplaced—take photographs of the damage and make a list of missing or damaged items.

In today's digital age, many interactions with law enforcement are recorded, either by dash cams, body cams, or by civilians using smartphones. If you or someone else recorded the encounter, ensure that the footage is saved securely. Back up digital files to multiple locations, such as cloud storage and external hard drives, to prevent loss. Do not edit or alter the recordings in any way, as unedited footage is more credible in legal contexts. If you believe law enforcement captured the incident on their recording devices, make a note to request access to this footage through a formal process later.

While it might be tempting to share your experience immediately on social media or with friends, it's wise to be cautious about public disclosures. Statements made publicly can be used against you or may inadvertently affect legal proceedings. Refrain from posting details about the encounter online until you've consulted with legal counsel. If you do discuss the incident, stick to factual accounts and avoid speculation or inflammatory language.

Seeking medical attention is advisable if you feel any physical or psychological effects from the encounter. Even if injuries seem minor, a professional medical evaluation can document your condition, which may be important evidence later. Stress and trauma can manifest in various ways, including anxiety, insomnia, or depression. Mental health professionals can provide support and treatment, and their records can also serve as documentation of the encounter's impact on your well-being.

Consulting with an attorney is a critical next step, especially if you believe your rights were violated or if you are facing potential charges. Legal counsel can guide you through the complexities of the legal system, advise you on how to protect yourself, and help you understand your options. They can assist in filing complaints, requesting evidence through formal channels, and representing you in court if necessary. Be honest and thorough when discussing the incident with your attorney; attorney-client privilege ensures that your conversations remain confidential.

Understanding that there are time-sensitive actions to consider is important. There may be deadlines for filing official complaints against law enforcement officers or agencies. For instance, some jurisdictions require that complaints be filed within a specific number of days after the incident. Missing these deadlines can limit your ability to seek redress. Your attorney can inform you of these time frames and help ensure that all necessary paperwork is completed promptly.

If you were issued a citation, summons, or notice to appear in court, it's imperative to address these promptly. Ignoring legal notices can result in additional charges, fines, or even warrants for your arrest. Carefully read any documents provided to you, note any court dates, and comply with all instructions. Your attorney can help you navigate these requirements and represent you in legal proceedings.

Throughout this process, it's essential to keep organized records. Create a dedicated file—physical or digital—where you store all documents related to the encounter. This includes your written account, photographs, medical records, legal documents, correspondence with attorneys, and any other relevant materials. Maintaining an organized record will facilitate smoother interactions with legal professionals and can be crucial if your case proceeds to court.

It's also beneficial to educate yourself about your rights and the legal remedies available to you. Resources are available through legal aid organizations, libraries, and reputable online platforms that can provide valuable information. Understanding the laws that govern police conduct and citizens' rights can empower you and help you make informed decisions.

Lastly, take care of your emotional well-being. Experiencing a police encounter can be traumatic, and it's important to address any emotional or psychological effects. Lean on trusted friends or family members for support, and consider speaking with a mental health professional if you're struggling to cope. Self-care is not only important for your personal health but can also help you remain focused and clear-headed as you navigate any legal processes ahead.

The immediate actions you take after a police encounter are critical in protecting your rights and interests. By calmly and methodically documenting the incident, preserving evidence, seeking legal counsel, and addressing any legal obligations promptly, you set a strong foundation for any necessary actions moving forward. Remember that while the encounter may have been distressing, you have agency in how you respond. Taking proactive, informed steps can help ensure that your rights are respected and that you are prepared for any challenges that may arise.

Navigating an Arrest

Being arrested is an experience that can evoke fear, confusion, and a sense of powerlessness. The sudden loss of freedom, the unfamiliar surroundings, and the uncertainty of what lies ahead can be overwhelming. However, understanding the arrest process and knowing your rights can empower you to navigate this challenging situation more effectively.

The moment of arrest is often abrupt. An officer may inform you that you are under arrest, perhaps placing handcuffs on your wrists and escorting you to a patrol car. It's important to remain calm and composed. Resisting arrest, even if you believe it to be unjustified, can lead to additional charges and complicate your legal situation. Remember that the side of the road or the scene of an incident is not the place to argue the merits of your case. Legal disputes are best resolved in court with the assistance of an attorney.

After your arrest, you will likely be transported to a police station or detention facility for booking. This process involves recording your personal information, such as your name, address, date of birth, and fingerprints. You may also have your photograph taken. The booking process formalizes your entry into the criminal justice system and creates an official record of your arrest. While it may feel invasive, cooperating during booking is generally in your best interest. Refusal to comply with booking procedures can lead to additional charges or complications.

During this time, law enforcement may attempt to question you about the incident leading to your arrest or other matters. It's important to reaffirm your decision to remain silent and request legal counsel if approached for questioning. In some cases, you may be placed in a holding cell with other detainees while awaiting further processing. This environment can be tense and unpredictable. It's advisable to keep to yourself, avoid engaging in conversations about your case or theirs, and remain as calm as possible. Your behavior during this time can impact how you are perceived by both law enforcement and the court.

Shortly after booking, you may have the opportunity to make a phone call. Use this opportunity wisely. Contact a trusted family member or friend who can help you secure legal representation or arrange for bail if applicable. Be mindful that phone calls from detention facilities are often recorded, so avoid discussing details of your case. Simply inform your contact of your situation and provide any necessary information for them to assist you.

The next step in the process is typically an arraignment or initial hearing, where you will appear before a judge. This hearing usually occurs within 48 to 72 hours of your arrest, excluding weekends and holidays. During the arraignment, the charges against you will be formally read, and you will have the opportunity to enter a plea of guilty, not guilty, or no contest. It's crucial to have legal representation by this point, as your attorney can advise you on the best course of action based on the specifics of your case.

At the arraignment, the judge will also address the issue of bail. Bail is a monetary guarantee paid to the court to ensure that you will appear at future court dates. The amount is typically determined based on factors such as the severity of the offense, your criminal history, ties to the community, and the risk of flight. Your attorney can advocate on your behalf for a reasonable bail amount or for release on your own recognizance, which allows you to be released without bail based on your promise to return to court.

If bail is set and you or your family can afford to pay it, you will be released from custody pending your next court appearance. If you cannot afford bail, your attorney may file a motion to reduce the bail amount or explore alternative options such as bail bonds or pretrial services programs. Remaining in custody can make it more challenging to prepare your defense, so exploring all avenues for release is important.

It is important to mention that the exact protocols, processes, and time frames associated with the judicial process can vary between jurisdictions and based on the severity of the crime. For example, someone who is arrested in the state of Ohio may have a different post-arrest experience than someone who is arrested in California.

Throughout this process, maintaining open and honest communication with your attorney is vital. Provide them with all relevant information, including your account of events, any evidence you believe may be helpful, and any concerns you have about the case. Remember that attorney-client privilege protects the confidentiality of your communications, allowing you to speak freely.

It's also important to comply with any conditions set by the court upon your release. This may include restrictions on travel, orders to refrain from contacting certain individuals, or requirements to check in regularly with a pretrial services officer. Violating these conditions can result in your re-arrest or having your bail revoked, meaning you would have to await trial in jail.

As your case progresses, your attorney will guide you through the legal proceedings, which may include preliminary hearings, plea negotiations, motions to suppress evidence, and potentially a trial. Stay engaged in your defense, attend all required court appearances, and follow your attorney's advice carefully.

Being arrested is a serious matter, but it's not insurmountable. Understanding the steps involved and exercising your rights can make a significant difference in the outcome of your case. By remaining calm, requesting legal counsel, and refraining from self-incrimination, you position yourself for the best possible defense. Remember that the legal system, while complex, is navigable with the right support and knowledge.

In addition to the legal aspects, take care of your personal well-being during this time. Reach out to supportive friends or family members, and consider seeking counseling if you're experiencing significant stress or anxiety. Managing your mental and emotional health is crucial as you work through the challenges ahead.

You should also consider taking time to reflect on the experience as an opportunity to learn and grow. Whether the arrest was the result of a misunderstanding, a momentary lapse in judgment, or circumstances beyond your control, use this time to consider your future steps carefully. Engage proactively with your attorney, stay informed about your case, and take the necessary actions to move forward positively.

Filing a Complaint

Experiencing a police encounter that leaves you feeling wronged, violated, or mistreated can be deeply unsettling. The sense of injustice may linger, prompting questions about how to hold the officers or the department accountable for their actions. Filing a formal complaint is a critical step in seeking redress and promoting accountability within law enforcement agencies. This process not only addresses your personal grievances but can also contribute to systemic improvements by highlighting areas where police conduct falls short. Understanding how to navigate the complaint process is essential for making your voice heard and effecting change.

Filing a complaint is a formal way to document the incident and initiate an internal review within the police department or an external oversight body. This process can lead to disciplinary actions against the officers involved, policy changes within the department, or even broader reforms in policing practices.

The first step in filing a complaint is to gather all relevant information about the incident. Reflect on the detailed notes and documentation you compiled immediately after the encounter. This includes the date, time, and location of the incident, the names and badge numbers of the officers involved, and a thorough account of what transpired. Objective, factual details are crucial; they lend credibility to your complaint and assist investigators in understanding the circumstances. If there were witnesses, their statements and contact information can strengthen your case. Photographs of injuries or property damage, medical reports, and any available video or audio recordings are valuable pieces of evidence.

Once you have organized your information, determine the appropriate entity to receive your complaint. Typically, complaints against police officers are filed with the internal affairs division of the respective law enforcement agency. Internal affairs units are responsible for investigating allegations of misconduct, corruption, or violations of department policies. Contact information for filing complaints is often available on the agency's official website or by calling their non-emergency number. Some departments provide online complaint forms or email addresses for submissions, while others may require in-person filings or mailed letters.

In certain jurisdictions, external oversight bodies exist to provide an additional layer of accountability. Civilian review boards or police oversight commissions are independent organizations tasked with investigating complaints against law enforcement. These bodies are designed to offer impartial reviews and may have the authority to make recommendations for disciplinary actions or policy changes. Research whether such an entity operates in your city or county and consider whether filing your complaint with them is appropriate.

When drafting your complaint, clarity and professionalism are paramount. Begin with a concise introduction stating your intent to file a formal complaint against specific officers or the department as a whole. Present the facts of the incident in a logical, chronological order, avoiding emotional language or personal attacks. Stick to objective descriptions of actions and statements, refraining from speculation about the officers' motives or intentions.

For example, instead of writing, "The officer rudely harassed me for no reason," you might state, "Officer Smith approached me at approximately 3:00 p.m. on Main Street and demanded to see my identification without providing a reason." This approach focuses on observable behaviors and interactions, allowing investigators to assess the situation based on verifiable facts.

In most cases you may choose to submit your complaint anonymously, however, if you intend to follow up your complaint with legal action, your identity will eventually be revealed to the officers anyway so this could be a waste of time and an unnecessary hurdle to jump through later. Although it may seem counterintuitive, providing your name and contact information along with your complaint is generally the best course of action. This allows the investigators to maintain contact with you throughout the investigation and ensures that your complaint is properly documented and can be easily referenced by a court if necessary.

If you are including supporting documents or evidence, reference them appropriately in your complaint. Indicate that you have attached photographs, witness statements, or recordings, and provide brief descriptions of their relevance. Ensure that all attachments are clearly labeled and organized for easy reference.

Before submitting your complaint, review it carefully for accuracy and completeness. Consider having a trusted friend, family member, or legal counsel read it to provide feedback. They may catch inconsistencies or suggest clarifications that strengthen your account. Remember that your complaint may become part of an official record and could be referenced in future legal proceedings, so it's important that it accurately reflects your experience.

After finalizing your complaint, make a copy of it for your own records and submit it according to the guidelines provided by the receiving agency. If mailing your complaint, use certified mail with a return receipt to confirm its delivery. Retain copies of all documents and correspondence for your records. If submitting electronically, save confirmation emails or screenshots that verify receipt.

Once your complaint is filed, the investigation process begins. The internal affairs division or oversight body will review your submission and determine the appropriate course of action. This may involve interviewing you, the officers involved, and any witnesses. They may also review body camera footage, dispatch records, and other relevant evidence. Investigations can take time, often weeks or months, depending on the complexity of the case and the workload of the investigative unit.

During this period, it's important to remain patient and cooperative. If investigators contact you for additional information or clarification, respond promptly and thoughtfully. Keep notes of all communications, including dates, times, and the names of investigators you speak with. This ongoing documentation can be valuable if questions arise about the handling of your complaint.

The outcome of the investigation may vary. If the investigators find that the officers violated department policies or laws, they may recommend disciplinary actions such as retraining, suspension, demotion, or termination. In some cases, the findings may lead to criminal charges. Alternatively, the investigation may conclude that the officers acted appropriately under the circumstances, or that there is insufficient evidence to substantiate your claims.

If you are dissatisfied with the outcome, you may have options for appeal or further action. Inquire about the agency's procedures for challenging the findings of an investigation. You might also consider seeking legal counsel to explore the possibility of filing a civil lawsuit against the officers or the department. An attorney can advise you on the merits of your case, the likelihood of success, and the potential remedies available, such as monetary damages or injunctive relief.

It's important to recognize that filing a complaint serves not only your personal interests but also the broader community. Patterns of misconduct often emerge through the accumulation of individual complaints, prompting departments to address systemic issues. Your willingness to come forward can contribute to greater accountability and improvements in policing practices.

Filing a complaint after a troubling police encounter is a

meaningful step toward seeking justice and promoting change. By approaching the process with preparation, professionalism, and persistence, you can effectively voice your concerns and hold law enforcement accountable for their actions. Remember that you are not alone in this journey, and resources are available to support you every step of the way.

Filing a FOIA Request

In the aftermath of a police encounter, information can be one of your most valuable assets. Understanding the specifics of what transpired, accessing official records, and obtaining documentation related to your case can significantly impact your ability to seek justice, protect your rights, and make informed decisions.

The 1966 Freedom of Information Act (FOIA) and its state equivalents provide a legal framework for citizens to request and obtain public records from government agencies. The Act was designed to promote transparency and accountability within government agencies by granting the public the right to access records and information. While FOIA specifically pertains to federal agencies, each state has its own version of this law, often referred to as Sunshine Laws, Public Records Acts, or Open Records Laws, that governs access to state and local government records, including those maintained by law enforcement agencies.

Understanding the scope of FOIA is essential. The act allows you to request existing records or documents that are in the possession of government agencies. This can include written reports, emails, photographs, audio and video recordings, policies, and more. It's important to note that FOIA does not require agencies to create new records in response to a request or to answer questions unrelated to existing documents. Therefore, crafting a clear and specific request is crucial to obtaining the information you seek.

To begin the process, identify the agency likely to possess the records relevant to your situation. If you're seeking records related to a local police encounter, the appropriate agency is typically the police department involved or the city's public records office. For state-level matters, you may need to contact the state police or relevant state agency. At the federal level, agencies such as the Federal Bureau of Investigation or the Department of Justice handle FOIA requests pertaining to their records.

Research the agency's specific procedures for submitting a FOIA request. Most agencies provide guidance on their websites, including contact information, submission methods, and any required forms. Some agencies accept requests via email or through online portals, while others may require mailed or faxed submissions. Understanding these requirements ensures that your request is properly received and processed.

When drafting your FOIA request, clarity and precision are paramount. Begin by addressing the request to the appropriate officer or department, such as the FOIA Officer or Public Records Custodian. Provide your full name and contact information, including your mailing address, phone number, and email address, so the agency can reach you with any questions or responses.

In the body of your request, clearly describe the records you are seeking. Be as specific as possible regarding dates, times, locations, incident numbers, involved parties, and types of documents. For example, you might write: "I am requesting copies of all police reports, body camera footage, dash camera recordings, dispatch logs, and any other records related to the traffic stop and arrest of [Your Name] on [Date] at approximately [Time] near the intersection of Main Street and First Avenue."

Providing detailed information helps the agency locate the records efficiently and may expedite your request. If you're uncertain about specific details, include any information you do have and indicate that you're seeking records related to a particular event or interaction. Avoid overly broad or vague requests, as these can result in delays or denials due to the burden they place on the agency.

Include a statement regarding your willingness to pay any applicable fees. Under FOIA, agencies are permitted to charge fees for search time, duplication, and review of records. You might write: "Please inform me of any fees exceeding [$Amount] before processing my request." Setting a fee limit allows you to control potential costs and decide whether to proceed if fees are higher than anticipated. In some cases, you may request a fee waiver, especially if the disclosure of the information is in the public interest and not primarily for commercial purposes. To request a waiver, provide a justification, explaining how the release of the information would contribute significantly to public understanding of government operations.

Be mindful of exemptions that may apply to your request. FOIA and state laws include specific exemptions that protect certain types of information from disclosure. Common exemptions relate to personal privacy, law enforcement proceedings, national security, and internal agency communications. For example, records that could interfere with an ongoing investigation or reveal confidential sources may be withheld. Understanding these exemptions can help you set realistic expectations and tailor your request accordingly. It may also be the case that you must be a resident of the state from which you are requesting records depending on the state's FOIA laws.

After completing your request, submit it according to the agency's guidelines. Keep a copy of your request and note the date of submission. Agencies are generally required to acknowledge receipt of your request and provide a response within a specific time frame, often within 10 to 20 business days. However, response times can vary based on the agency, the complexity of your request, and the volume of requests they handle. In some cases, agencies may invoke extensions due to unusual circumstances.

Upon receiving a response, review it carefully. The agency may provide the requested records in full, partially, or deny the request entirely. If records are withheld or redacted, the agency should cite the specific exemptions or reasons for the denial. If you receive a denial or are dissatisfied with the response, you have the right to appeal the decision. The agency's response should include information on the appeals process, including deadlines and where to send your appeal.

Crafting an effective appeal involves addressing the reasons for the denial and providing arguments for why the records should be released. You may challenge the application of exemptions, clarify misunderstandings, or provide additional context. Submitting a well-reasoned appeal can result in a reversal of the initial decision or, at the very least, a more detailed explanation of the agency's position.

If your appeal is unsuccessful, you may consider pursuing

legal action. Consulting with an attorney experienced in public records law can help you assess the merits of your case and navigate the complexities of litigation. Lawsuits can be time-consuming and costly, so weighing the potential benefits against the resources required is important.

It's also valuable to be aware of state-specific nuances in public records laws. While the general principles are similar, each state has its own statutes, procedures, and exemptions. Some states have more expansive definitions of public records, while others have more restrictive provisions. Resources such as the state's attorney general's office, legal aid organizations, or public interest groups can provide guidance on navigating state laws.

Throughout the FOIA process, maintaining organized records of all correspondence and communications is crucial. Keep copies of your requests, confirmations of receipt, agency responses, and any notes from phone conversations. This documentation can be essential if disputes arise or if you need to demonstrate compliance with procedural requirements.

In addition to obtaining records for your personal case, FOIA can be a powerful tool for promoting transparency and accountability in government operations more broadly. Journalists, researchers, and advocacy groups frequently use FOIA requests to uncover information of public significance, leading to reforms, policy changes, or increased public awareness. By exercising your right to access public records, you contribute to the democratic principle of an informed citizenry.

Remember that patience and persistence are often necessary when navigating the FOIA process. Delays and obstacles can be frustrating, but understanding the system and remaining committed to your objectives can yield valuable information. Stay informed about your rights under the law, seek assistance when needed, and approach the process with diligence. Filing a FOIA request empowers you to access information that can be critical in addressing the aftermath of a police encounter.

By understanding the legal framework, crafting precise requests, and navigating the procedural steps effectively, you can obtain records that support your pursuit of justice and accountability. Knowledge is a powerful ally, and utilizing the tools available to you strengthens your ability to advocate for yourself and contribute to a transparent and accountable society.

Seeking Legal Representation

After a challenging encounter with law enforcement, especially ones that may involve potential legal consequences or violations of your rights, one of the most critical steps you can take is to secure competent legal representation. An experienced attorney can provide invaluable guidance, protect your interests, and help you navigate the complex legal landscape that follows such incidents.

The legal system is intricate and often intimidating for those unfamiliar with its workings. Laws vary by jurisdiction, procedures can be convoluted, and the stakes are often high. Attempting to manage legal matters on your own can lead to missteps that may adversely affect the outcome of your case. An attorney brings expertise, strategic insight, and an objective perspective that is essential for advocating on your behalf. Whether you are facing criminal charges, considering a civil lawsuit, or seeking to hold law enforcement accountable for misconduct, legal counsel is a crucial ally.

Understanding the importance of legal representation begins with recognizing the role an attorney plays. They serve as your advocate, advisor, and negotiator. An attorney will assess the facts of your case, identify legal issues, and develop strategies tailored to your specific circumstances. They can communicate effectively with prosecutors, opposing counsel, and the court, ensuring that your rights are protected at every stage. Additionally, an attorney can help you understand the potential outcomes, risks, and benefits of different courses of action, allowing you to make informed decisions with confidence.

It is important to reiterate that you have a right to a public defender if you cannot afford to hire your own legal representation, and you should never waive your right to a public defender unless you intend to find your own attorney. Public defenders handle everything from advising clients, negotiating plea deals, gathering evidence, and representing them in court, and they can be a powerful tool for those who cannot afford private representation. It is worth noting that public defenders are only available for criminal offenses, not traffic infractions or civil lawsuits.

Finding the right attorney requires careful consideration. Not all lawyers have the same areas of expertise, and selecting one who is experienced in the relevant field is essential. For matters involving police encounters, civil rights violations, or criminal charges, you may seek attorneys who specialize in criminal defense, civil rights law, or personal injury law, depending on the specifics of your situation. Begin your search by asking for recommendations from trusted friends or family members who have had positive experiences with legal professionals. Personal referrals can provide insight into an attorney's competence, communication style, and dedication.

If personal referrals are not available, consider utilizing resources such as local bar association directories, online legal referral services, or legal aid organizations. Many bar associations offer lawyer referral programs that connect individuals with attorneys who have the appropriate expertise. Online platforms often allow you to search for attorneys based on practice areas, location, and client reviews. Legal aid organizations can provide low-cost or pro bono services to individuals who meet certain income criteria, ensuring that financial limitations do not prevent access to legal representation.

Once you have identified potential attorneys, conduct preliminary research to assess their qualifications. Review their professional websites, paying attention to their educational background, years of experience, areas of specialization, and any notable case results or accolades. Look for indications of their commitment to clients, such as testimonials or endorsements. Verify their standing with the state bar association to ensure they are licensed to practice law and have not faced disciplinary actions. This due diligence helps you narrow down your choices to attorneys who are both competent and trustworthy.

Scheduling consultations with prospective attorneys is a critical next step. Many attorneys offer initial consultations at little or no cost, providing an opportunity to discuss your case and evaluate whether they are the right fit for your needs. Prepare for these meetings by organizing all relevant documents and information related to your case. This may include police reports, correspondence, photographs, medical records, witness statements, and any other evidence you have collected. Bringing a comprehensive file allows the attorney to assess your situation more accurately and offer meaningful insights.

During the consultation, communicate openly and honestly about the details of your encounter with law enforcement. Transparency is vital, as withholding information can hinder the attorney's ability to represent you effectively. Discuss your objectives and concerns, whether they involve defending against criminal charges, seeking compensation for damages, or pursuing policy changes. Ask questions to gauge the attorney's experience with similar cases, their proposed strategies, and their approach to client communication. Understanding how they plan to handle your case and how they interact with clients can help you determine if they align with your expectations.

Inquire about the attorney's fee structure to ensure that their services are financially feasible for you. Attorneys may charge hourly rates, flat fees, or work on a contingency basis, where they receive a percentage of any settlement or judgment awarded. Clarify what expenses are included in their fees and whether additional costs may arise, such as filing fees, expert witness fees, or administrative expenses. Understanding the financial aspects upfront prevents surprises later and allows you to plan accordingly.

Evaluate not only the attorney's qualifications but also your comfort level with them. A strong attorney-client relationship is built on trust, respect, and effective communication. You should feel confident in their abilities and comfortable discussing sensitive information. Pay attention to how well they listen to your concerns, whether they explain legal concepts clearly, and if they demonstrate empathy for your situation. An attorney who is attentive and responsive is more likely to provide the support and advocacy you need during this challenging time.

Once you have made your decision, formalize the relationship by signing a retainer agreement or engagement letter. This document outlines the scope of the attorney's services, fee arrangements, and other essential terms of the representation. Reviewing this agreement carefully ensures that both you and the attorney have a clear understanding of expectations. Throughout your engagement with your attorney, maintain open lines of communication. Provide updates on any new developments related to your case and promptly respond to requests for information.

Likewise, expect your attorney to keep you informed about progress, deadlines, and important decisions. If you have questions or concerns, do not hesitate to raise them.

An effective attorney-client relationship is collaborative, with both parties working toward a common goal. Be mindful of your obligations as a client. Attend all scheduled meetings and court appearances, adhere to legal advice, and avoid actions that could jeopardize your case. This includes refraining from discussing your case publicly or on social media, as statements made outside the attorney-client privilege can be used against you. Trust in your attorney's expertise, but also take an active role in understanding the legal processes involved. Educating yourself empowers you to make informed decisions and contributes to a more effective partnership.

In some instances, you may encounter challenges with your attorney, such as disagreements over strategy, communication issues, or concerns about performance. If problems arise, address them directly with your attorney to seek resolution. Open dialogue can often resolve misunderstandings or clarify expectations. However, if issues persist and you believe they impede your representation, you have the right to seek alternative counsel. Transitioning to a new attorney should be handled carefully to minimize disruptions to your case.

Securing legal representation is a significant step toward protecting your rights and achieving a favorable outcome. An attorney serves as both a shield and a guide, navigating the complexities of the legal system on your behalf. By investing time and effort into finding the right attorney and fostering a strong working relationship, you enhance your ability to face the challenges ahead with confidence.

Remember that the legal process can be lengthy and may require patience and resilience. Trust in your attorney's guidance, stay engaged in your case, and focus on the steps within your control. Surround yourself with a support network of friends and family who can offer encouragement and assistance. Taking care of your emotional and physical well-being is essential during this time.

Seeking legal representation after a police encounter is a critical component of asserting your rights and navigating the path toward justice. By understanding the importance of legal counsel, diligently selecting an attorney who aligns with your needs, and actively participating in your defense, you empower yourself to face the legal system with greater assurance. Knowledge, preparation, and partnership with a skilled attorney are key elements in transforming a daunting experience into an opportunity for resolution, growth, and justice.

Understanding Police Liability

Beyond filing complaints or seeking disciplinary action against individual officers, you may wonder how to hold the police department or municipality accountable for the harm you've suffered. Understanding the legal avenues available for pursuing civil action against law enforcement agencies is essential for asserting your rights and seeking compensation.

When considering legal action against a police department or municipality, it's important to grasp the foundational principle that governmental entities can, under certain circumstances, be held liable for the actions of their employees. This concept is rooted in the idea that public institutions have a responsibility to ensure that their agents adhere to constitutional standards and that failures in training, supervision, or policy can result in harm to citizens. Pursuing a civil lawsuit not only seeks compensation for your individual damages but can also serve as a catalyst for institutional change.

One of the primary legal frameworks for holding police accountable is found in federal law, specifically 42 U.S.C. § 1983, commonly referred to as Section 1983. As mentioned in chapter one, this statute allows individuals to file lawsuits against government officials, including police officers, who have violated their constitutional rights under color of law. Under Section 1983, you can allege that an officer's actions infringed upon your rights protected by the Constitution, such as the Fourth Amendment's protection against unreasonable searches and seizures or the First Amendment's protection of free speech. However, navigating a Section 1983 claim involves overcoming significant legal hurdles, one of which is the doctrine of qualified immunity.

Qualified immunity is a judicially created doctrine that shields government officials from personal liability for civil damages, provided their conduct did not violate "clearly established" statutory or constitutional rights of which a reasonable person would have known. This means that even if an officer infringed upon your rights, they may be immune from liability unless it can be shown that their actions contravened established legal precedent.

The qualified immunity defense poses a substantial challenge in civil rights litigation. Courts often require that the violated right be defined with a high degree of specificity, which can make it difficult to establish that the officer's conduct was clearly unlawful in the context of previous cases. Nonetheless, recent legal developments and growing public scrutiny have sparked debates about the application of qualified immunity, leading some courts to re-examine its boundaries. Understanding this doctrine is crucial for assessing the viability of your claim and strategizing with your attorney on how to address it.

In addition to suing individual officers, you may pursue claims against the municipality or police department itself. Under the Supreme Court's decision in Monell v. Department of Social Services, local governments can be held liable under Section 1983 when the constitutional violation results from an official policy, practice, or custom. This means that if you can demonstrate that the misconduct was a result of departmental policies, inadequate training, or deliberate indifference to constitutional rights, the municipality may be held responsible.

Proving municipal liability requires a thorough investigation into the department's practices. This may involve uncovering patterns of similar misconduct, demonstrating failures in training programs, or revealing that superiors were aware of but ignored systemic issues. Such claims are complex and often require extensive legal expertise and resources. However, successful litigation can lead to substantial settlements or judgments, compelling the municipality to implement reforms to prevent future violations.

When a lawsuit is filed against a police department or municipality, the prospect of a settlement often arises. Settlements are agreements reached between the parties to resolve the dispute without proceeding to a full trial. From the municipality's perspective, settling a case can avoid the costs of litigation, the uncertainty of a jury verdict, and potential negative publicity. For plaintiffs, settlements provide a guaranteed outcome and can expedite compensation.

Cities and municipalities typically have insurance policies or budget allocations specifically designated for legal settlements involving police misconduct. These funds are used to pay for legal defenses and to satisfy settlement agreements or court judgments. The existence of such budgets acknowledges the reality that lawsuits are a foreseeable consequence of police operations. However, critics argue that when settlements are paid from public funds, there may be insufficient financial incentive for departments to address underlying issues, as individual officers or officials rarely bear personal financial responsibility.

The impact of settlements extends beyond the immediate parties involved. High-profile cases or those resulting in substantial payouts can draw public attention to systemic problems within a police department. This scrutiny can prompt policy reviews, legislative action, or changes in leadership. In some instances, settlement agreements may include nonmonetary terms, such as commitments to implement specific reforms, enhance training programs, or engage in community oversight. These provisions can be instrumental in driving meaningful change.

Pursuing civil action requires careful consideration and preparation. Consulting with an attorney experienced in civil rights litigation is essential. They can evaluate the merits of your case, advise you on the potential challenges, and develop a strategic approach tailored to your circumstances. Your attorney will help you gather evidence, identify expert witnesses, and navigate procedural requirements. They will also handle negotiations with the municipality's legal representatives and advocate on your behalf throughout the legal process.

It's important to be aware that civil litigation can be lengthy and emotionally taxing. The discovery process, where both sides exchange information and evidence, can be invasive and time-consuming. Depositions may require you to recount traumatic experiences in detail. The defense may attempt to challenge your credibility or minimize the severity of the misconduct. Preparing yourself mentally and emotionally for these aspects is crucial. Moreover, the outcome of litigation is never guaranteed. Courts may dismiss claims based on legal technicalities, procedural issues, or interpretations of the law. Settlements may not fully compensate for the harm you've suffered, and the desire for systemic change may not be immediately realized. Nonetheless, pursuing legal action can be a powerful statement of resistance against injustice and can contribute to the broader movement for police accountability.

In addition to federal claims under Section 1983, state laws may provide alternative or supplementary avenues for relief.

Many states have statutes that allow for lawsuits based on assault, battery, false arrest, or negligence by law enforcement officers. State tort claims can sometimes circumvent certain immunities that apply in federal court, although they may present their own set of challenges and limitations. Your attorney can advise you on the most appropriate jurisdiction and legal grounds for your case.

It's also worth noting that legislative efforts are underway in some jurisdictions to reform laws related to police liability. Movements to limit or abolish qualified immunity, enhance transparency, and increase accountability are gaining momentum. Staying informed about these developments can provide context for your case and may influence legal strategies or the likelihood of success. Remember that your pursuit of justice is not only for yourself but can also pave the way for others who have faced similar injustices.

Understanding police liability and the mechanisms of settlements is a critical component of responding effectively to police misconduct. By recognizing the legal principles that govern these actions, such as qualified immunity and municipal liability under Section 1983, you can make informed decisions about pursuing civil remedies. There have been many instances where citizens seeking justice for police misconduct has created significant change in the landscape of civilian rights, as demonstrated by the cases highlighted in this book. While the path may be challenging, holding law enforcement accountable through the legal system can lead to personal vindication, compensation for your losses, and contribute to meaningful changes that enhance justice and equity in policing practices.

Resources for Deeper Understanding

In the journey to protect your rights and navigate interactions with law enforcement effectively, knowledge is your most potent tool. Understanding the legal system, your constitutional protections, and the mechanisms available for redress not only empowers you personally but also contributes to a more informed and just society. While this book provides a foundational overview, delving deeper into legal education can enhance your confidence and competence in handling future encounters. The legal landscape is vast and multifaceted, encompassing statutes, case law, procedural rules, and constitutional principles that govern every aspect of society.

For many, the law can seem opaque and intimidating, filled with complex terminology and intricate doctrines. However, the democratization of information in the digital age has made legal knowledge more accessible than ever before. By taking advantage of available resources, you can demystify the law and gain insights that were once confined to legal professionals.

One of the most immediate and accessible resources for legal education is your local public library and state or county law library. Libraries often house extensive collections of legal texts, including guides written specifically for non-lawyers. These materials cover a range of topics, from understanding your rights during police encounters to navigating the court system. Librarians can assist you in locating relevant books and may even offer access to legal databases that provide up-to-date statutes and case law. Engaging with these resources allows you to explore legal concepts at your own pace, in a setting conducive to focused learning.

In addition to physical books, the internet offers a wealth of information tailored to laypersons seeking legal knowledge. Reputable websites, such as those maintained by legal aid organizations, bar associations, and government agencies, provide comprehensive guides, FAQs, and instructional materials. For example, the American Civil Liberties Union offers resources on civil rights and liberties, while the National Association of Criminal Defense Lawyers provides insights into criminal justice issues. These organizations strive to make legal information accessible and actionable, empowering individuals to understand and assert their rights.

Online legal platforms, such as FindLaw, Nolo, and Justia, offer articles, blogs, and forums where legal topics are discussed in plain language. These sites often include glossaries of legal terms, explanations of legal procedures, and guides on specific issues like filing a lawsuit or responding to a subpoena. While these resources should not substitute for professional legal advice, they can enhance your foundational understanding and help you formulate informed questions when consulting with an attorney.

Educational institutions also play a significant role in promoting public legal education. Community colleges and universities may offer courses or workshops designed for non-lawyers interested in learning about the legal system. Continuing education programs often include classes on constitutional law, criminal justice, and civil rights. Enrolling in such courses provides structured learning opportunities led by knowledgeable instructors, fostering a deeper comprehension of legal principles. Additionally, some law schools host public lectures, seminars, or clinics that are open to community members, allowing you to engage directly with legal scholars and practitioners.

Another avenue for legal education is participation in community organizations focused on justice and reform. Joining local chapters of civil rights groups, such as the NAACP, the Legal Aid Society, or grassroots advocacy organizations, connects you with like-minded individuals committed to legal empowerment. These groups frequently hold workshops, training sessions, and discussion forums where members can learn about legal issues affecting their communities.

Engaging with the legislative process is another powerful way to deepen your legal understanding. By following the development of laws at the local, state, or federal level, you gain insights into how statutes are created and amended. Attending city council meetings, legislative hearings, or town halls allows you to observe lawmakers in action and understand the factors influencing legal decisions. Many government bodies provide live streams or recordings of these sessions, making them accessible regardless of your location. Becoming informed about pending legislation can also enable you to advocate for laws that protect and advance civil liberties.

Podcasts, webinars, and online lectures have become increasingly popular mediums for legal education. Legal experts and scholars often share their insights through these platforms, discussing contemporary legal issues, landmark cases, and practical advice. Programs like "Radiolab's More Perfect," which explores the history and impact of Supreme Court decisions, or "Justice in America," which delves into the criminal justice system, offer engaging and informative content accessible to a general audience. Listening to these discussions can broaden your perspective and keep you informed about current legal debates.

For those interested in a more interactive approach, moot court competitions or mock trials offer experiential learning opportunities. While traditionally associated with law students, some community organizations and educational institutions host simulations open to the public. Participating in these events allows you to step into the roles of attorneys, witnesses, or jurors, gaining firsthand experience with legal procedures and argumentation. Such activities can demystify the courtroom environment and enhance your analytical and rhetorical skills.

Legal self-help centers are another valuable resource, particularly for individuals who may need to represent themselves in legal matters. These centers, often affiliated with courts or legal aid organizations, provide materials, forms, and guidance on navigating the legal system. Staffed by knowledgeable personnel, they can assist you in understanding court procedures, filing documents, and accessing legal services. While they do not offer legal advice, they can help you navigate administrative aspects and connect you with additional resources.

It's important to approach legal education with a critical and discerning mindset. While the abundance of information available is beneficial, not all sources are equally reliable. Prioritize resources from reputable organizations, verified legal professionals, and official government publications. Be cautious of information found on unofficial blogs, forums, or social media posts that may contain inaccuracies or personal opinions presented as fact. Cross-referencing information across multiple credible sources can help ensure that your understanding is accurate and current.

As you expand your legal knowledge, consider how you can apply it to real-world situations. Reflect on past experiences with law enforcement or the legal system, analyzing them through the lens of your newfound understanding. This reflection can reveal areas where you might have acted differently or can inform your approach in future interactions. Sharing your knowledge with others in your community can also amplify its impact, fostering a more informed and empowered populace.

Understanding the legal system is not only about reacting to encounters with law enforcement but also about proactive engagement with your rights and responsibilities as a citizen. Knowledge equips you to advocate effectively for yourself and others, to participate meaningfully in civic processes, and to contribute to the pursuit of justice. It demystifies institutions that may otherwise seem inaccessible and provides tools to challenge injustices when they arise. In cultivating legal literacy, patience and persistence are key. The law is a complex and evolving field, and mastery takes time. Set realistic goals for your learning journey, and acknowledge the progress you make along the way. Engage with others who share your interest, as collaborative learning can enhance comprehension and provide mutual support.

Always bear in mind that while self-education is invaluable, it does not replace professional legal counsel when needed. Complex legal issues, particularly those involving potential litigation or criminal charges, require the expertise of qualified attorneys. Use your knowledge to inform your interactions with legal professionals, enabling you to ask pertinent questions and understand the advice provided.

Empowering yourself through legal education is a proactive step toward navigating the challenges that may arise in interactions with law enforcement and the broader legal system. Knowledge is not only a personal asset but a collective one, strengthening the fabric of society through informed and engaged citizens. Embrace the opportunities to learn, grow, and contribute, knowing that your efforts make a meaningful and practical difference in your life and the lives of those around you.

If you're interested in learning more and seeing how the concepts we discussed in this book play out in everyday real life, then I highly encourage you to check out the Audit the Audit YouTube channel by scanning the QR code below.

Made in United States
Troutdale, OR
12/11/2024